Preface

COVID-19 has stirred the lives of many across the world. This epidemic has been upgraded to Pandemic on 11 March 2020 by WHO. In its initial period (i.e. during January 2020), besides China, COVID-19 had alerted only the neighbouring ASEAN countries, Taiwan, HK and Japan. Other countries have been watching from the sidelines the new cases being reported in the south-east Asian countries. Authorities in Asian regions worked hard to contain the spread till Mid-March 2020.

Authorities in remaining countries were caught off guard. Most of other countries downplayed the infectiousness of this disease. By March, Europe felt the brunt of this Pandemic and in a few weeks, it engulfed entire European regions with a severe level of infection and mortality rate than what we witnessed in Asia. Then it struck the US regions with even a higher infection rate than Europe but with a bit lower mortality rate. Then it wreaked havoc in South America, India and Africa.

For many people, it turned out to be a calamity of unprecedented magnitude. People have been forced by this virus to remain stuck at home. People's lifestyle has changed drastically during the containment period because of the constant fear of getting infected. People are glued to websites that publish the daily infection number. Many of us are keen to see the flattening of infection rate curve at the earliest.

Virus is still wracking the havoc even after 6 months of its origination. There are no vaccines in the sight for the next few months though more than 100 candidates are toiling to get lucky. There is a higher likelihood of arrival of a second wave of this Pandemic as happened during all previous Pandemic (Spanish flu, Asian Flu and Hong Kong Flu). Second wave in all previous Pandemics was more severe than the first wave.

There are so many unknowns about the life during and after this Pandemic. There are so many unknowns for the policy makers. There is a trade-off for the policymakers to either save the economy from freefall or contain the Pandemic, save important lives and prevent further transmission.

Each passing day, during this Pandemic, has an economic cost associated with it.

This book attempts to provide a ground reality of this Pandemic from Socio-economic standpoint. It tries to assess the economic cost of this Pandemic for different regions across the globe. It also tries to delve deeper into the recent history (not too far away from the present) of past 100 years and analyse the socio-economic impact of past pandemics. Impact of previous pandemic may not be perfectly correlated with the prevailing 2020 COVID-19 Pandemic, but the history does provide a good baseline to understand the consequences of such Pandemics.

ORGANIZATION OF THE BOOK

The book has been organized into six chapters. A brief description of each of the chapters are as follows:

Chapter 1: Economic Cost of 2020 Pandemic

Provides a detailed background of COVID-19 background, its origination and its family of strains. After the COVID-19 background, there is an analysis of economic cost of the COVID-19 across the world (split into 3 broader categories: Global impact, Impact on Advanced economies and Impact on Emerging and developing economies). This analysis is based on 2 broader parameters – Direct Impact (GDP growth rate) and Potential Impact (GINI index, %Informal employment & HAQ Index).

Chapter 2: Policy Response to COVID-19 - US

Presents a detailed overview of the impact of COVID-19 on US, level of containment measures undertaken by US authorities, Fiscal Policy responses and Monetary Policy responses.

Chapter 3: Policy Response to COVID-19 - Europe

Presents a detailed overview of the impact of COVID-19 on Major European countries, level of containment measures undertaken by European countries, Fiscal Policy responses and Monetary Policy responses.

Chapter 4: Policy Response to COVID-19 - Emerging Markets economies (EM)

Presents a detailed overview of the impact of COVID-19 on selected Emerging Markets economies (EM), level of containment measures undertaken by EM countries, Fiscal Policy responses and Monetary Policy responses.

Chapter 5: Economic Lessons from Past Pandemics

Presents a holistic overview of 3 past Pandemics (1918 Spanish flu, 1957 Asian flu and 1968 Hong Kong Flu). It does a collection review of impact of all 3 pandemic on stock indices, Mortality rate at global level, classification of Pandemic into different severity level & expected impact of each such Pandemic on different regions across the globe.

Then, for each of the 3 Pandemics, it reviews its Origin, virus family, Mutation details, Historical background behind the Pandemic name, Infection rate, mortality rate, how and when Pandemic ended, long term societal impact of the Pandemic, Economic impact of the Pandemic on various regions across the globe and detailed impact on stock markets.

Chapter 6: Success Stories of Response to COVID-19

There have been numerous success stories related to response to COVID-19. But this chapter attempts to reviews the response of 3 nations (whose response stands out from the other country) – Taiwan, New Zealand and Germany.

Chapter-1

Economic cost of 2020 Pandemic

- About COVID-19
- Economic Cost of COVID-19
    a. Direct Cost
        i. GDP Growth rate
    b. Potential Cost
        i. GINI Index (to measure inequality)
        ii. Percentage of Informal employment
        iii. HAQ Index (Healthcare Access & Quality Index)

About COVID-19

2020 COVID-19 Pandemic is being compared with 1918 Spanish flu Pandemic in its severity. It has been found to be much more severe than the previous two Pandemics – 1957 Asian Flu and 1968 Hong Kong Flu Pandemic (More details on the past Pandemic and its economic cost in later chapters).

COVID-19 strain (genetic variant or subtype of a micro-organism or Virus) is believed to have originated from its first host, Bats near Wuhan (China). These Bats hold a mix of coronavirus strains. During early December 2019, one of the strains, opportunistic enough to cross species lines, left its host and ended up in a person. Since then, it is wracking havoc across the world.

Severe acute respiratory syndrome coronavirus 2 (SARS-CoV-2) is the strain of coronavirus that causes coronavirus (COVID-19) disease. This coronavirus strain is a member of the severe acute respiratory syndrome coronavirus. It has been classified as a Positive-sense single-stranded RNA virus. The positive-sense RNA genome (genetic material of the organism) can serve as messenger RNA and can be translated into protein in the host cell. SARS-CoV-2 and SARS-CoV strains are quite similar. The spike protein of SARS-CoV-2 (SARS-2-S) is 76% identical with SARS-S.

Positive-sense RNA viruses account for a large fraction of known viruses, including many pathogens (an infectious or biological agent that causes disease or illness to its host) such as the hepacivirus C (hepatitis C virus belongs this family), West Nile virus, dengue virus, SARS & MERS coronaviruses, and SARS-CoV-2 as well as less clinically serious pathogens such as the rhinoviruses that cause the common cold.

Epidemiologists believe that each COVID-19 infection results in 1.4 - 3.9 new ones if no preventive measures taken. The virus primarily transmits between people through close contact and through respiratory droplets produced after coughs or sneezes.

This COVID-19 virus is perceived to be deadly because of two factors – its easy transmissibility traits and being non-symptomatic in many cases.

There has been almost exponential growth in infection cases across the world within less than 3 months of identification of its first case in Wuhan.

"This is a distinct and very new situation," says epidemiologist Sarah Cobey of the University of Chicago.

Economic Cost of COVID-19 Pandemic

COVID-19 Pandemic has done an unprecedented damage to global economy in 2020. A major part of the economic activities has been disrupted because of imposition of the containment measures in majority of countries across the world.

Impact of COVID-19 can be measured in 2 ways – One is the **direct economic cost**, which can be measured directly from the expected drop in GDP growth rate across the world and the other is the **Indirect or Potential economic cost,** which we can gauge by assessing the country's current standing on 3 crucial parameters - GINI Index , % Informal employment and HAQ Index:

1. Direct Cost - **GDP Growth rate**
2. Indirect Cost - **GINI Index** (to measure inequality)
3. Indirect Cost - **% Informal employment** (to measure the adverse impact of containment measures on the daily wage earners)
4. Indirect Cost - **HAQ Index** (Healthcare Access & Quality Index; to measure the existing hospital infrastructure of affected countries)

In order to get a generic view of economic impact on global economy, we must review each of the above four parameters for 3 sub-groups – Global economy, Advanced Economies (G7 and other developed countries) and Emerging Markets & Developing countries.

Direct cost is something which can be forecasted by assessing the drop in GDP growth. This assessment is based on impact to formalised segment of economy. But it fails to gauge the impact on the economy because of Informal segments.

So, we must complement our assessment by considering the **% of informal segments of economy.** Impact due to informal segment does not get formally captured as economic cost and it is a potential cost, which has not been accounted for. So, we are tracking it under "Indirect Cost" category.

The **GINI Index** tracks the existing level of income inequality in the economy. The worst is the performance of a country on **GINI Index** parameter, the more is impact on its citizens. But this cost will be tracked under "Indirect Cost" category because it is a potential cost and has not been accounted for.

HAQ index tracks the existing robustness of the country's healthcare and its quality to control non-pandemic related diseases. An inefficient and inadequate healthcare system, which can hardly control the non-pandemic related curable diseases, is expected to magnify the impact of incurable diseases (COVID-19) on its citizens.

Direct Economic Cost

GDP Growth Rate

We understand the limitation of using GDP (Gross development Product) for measuring the economic performance of a country. –
- GDP fails to measure the welfare activities.
- GDP only includes market transactions.
- GDP fails to measure the income distribution.
- GDP does not care about what is being produced.
- GDP ignores the externalities in its y-o-y or q-o-q number.

But still GDP is most reliable indicator of economy's size of a country. The GDP growth rate is the most widely used indicator of economic growth of a country.

A country's GDP represents the total value of goods and services produced within a country's borders in a specific time frame — quarterly or annually.

Why is GDP growth rate so important?

- GDP growth rate gives an outlook for revenue (tax collections) growth for the Government. It provides a base for the government to plan its annual budget.
- A higher GDP growth rate signals a good revenue growth for the corporates.
- For Salaried class, it acts as an impetus for the wage growth.
- If GDP growth rate falls below the borrowing rate of a country, then it is likely to affect the sovereign credit rating of the country. It also results in further borrowing becoming costlier for the government.
- It is used by central bank to gauge the economic cycle of the economy. If GDP growth is too high and above its potential, then interest rate is recommended to move up else it is recommended to cut down.

- When GDP growth rate is positive and higher than same quarter last year, the economy is generally thought to be doing well. A weak growth signals that the economy is not doing well.
- If nominal GDP is less than same quarter last year, then GDP growth is negative for that quarter. It usually represents the falling incomes, lower consumption and higher employment rate (or job-loss). The economy is in recession when there are two consecutive quarters of negative GDP growth.
- For common man, a lower GDP translates into a proportionate decline in per capita income. Further, for economy where inequality (distribution of wealth) is higher, it is very likely that the poor will suffer more from the drop in the GDP growth rate than the rich.
- In 1962, Arthur Okun, staff economist for U.S. President John F. Kennedy's Council of Economic Advisers, coins **Okun's Law**. As per this law, for every 3-point rise in GDP, unemployment will fall 1 percentage point. The theory guides US monetary policy.

Impact of COVID-19 on GDP Growth – World Economy

COVID-19 has stalled the economic activities across the world, because of the containment measures adopted by various countries. So, it was quite evident that the GDP growth, during the next few quarters in this financial year, will get adversely impacted. It was just a matter of quantifying the extent of drop in GDP growth rate.

Below is historical annual GDP growth rate of World Economy since 2007. Blue coloured bar indicates the actual figure of GDP growth rate and how global economy was doing just before COVID-19 pandemic since 2007. While the light orange coloured bar is the IMF projected GDP Growth rate for 2020 and 2021.

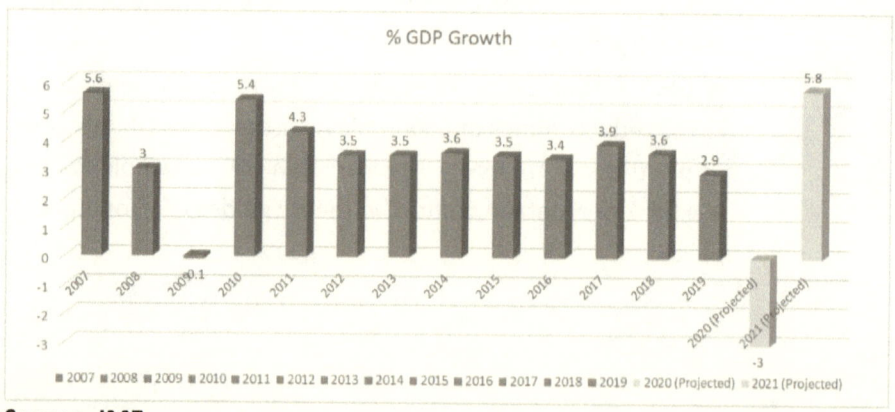

Source: IMF

The above historical GDP Growth rate chart encompasses two major economic crisis - 2008-09 global financial crisis (GFC) and 2020 COVID-19 Pandemic.

When GFC had hit us, the global growth rate was averaging at a healthy rate of 5% level. GFC impact was not immediate on World economy. It took 2 years to see the decline in GDP Growth rate from average GDP growth rate of 5%+ to below zero growth rate (-0.1%). It is estimated that every 1% GDP growth loss in the global GDP resulted in 14 million addition into poverty zone (major chunks of them in emerging markets & developing economies).

Fall in GDP growth rate i.e. Recession also causes expansion of the informal sector in the economy. Global growth rebounded sharply in 2010(a year after GFC crisis) to pre-GFC growth rate of above 5%. But average growth rate couldn't reach the pre-COVID19 level of 5%+ rate after GFC. Reason of sudden spike in GDP in 2010(to 5.4% from 0.1%) was huge economic stimulus measures undertaken globally by most of the countries.

IMF had advised all countries to have at least 2% of country's GDP as stimulus packages to support the economy from further contraction. Most of such plans were based on Keynesian theory of deficit spending (increase the fiscal deficit for few years to support the fall in demand by Govt spending). Reason for lower average growth rate (3.5%) after 2012 onwards was the fiscal consolidation measures undertaken by many countries to reduce the debt (piled up since GFC crisis) and fiscal deficit in a phased manner.

When COVID-19 hit us in January 2020, the global GDP growth rate was stabilising at 3.5% level. But just a year before this crisis (i.e. in 2019), the global growth was already in slowdown phase (a fall of 0.6% from average growth rate 3.5%). In order to fight the slowdown, many countries started monetary policy easing in the 2nd half of 2019. It resulted in adding additional 0.5% growth in 2019 and expected to add additional 0.5% to 2020 growth rate (had COVID-19 didn't happen).

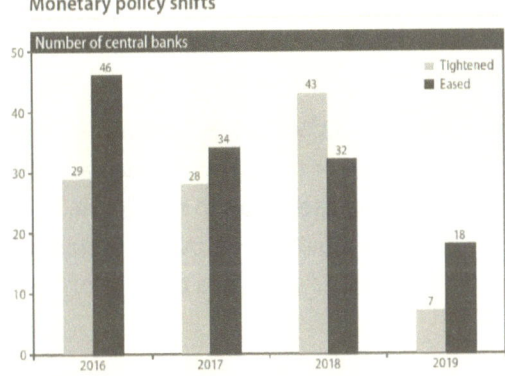

Figure 1
Monetary policy shifts

Source: Central Bank News.
Note: As of 29 April 2019. Sample covers 95 central banks across developed and developing economies, as well as the economies in transition.

US Fed's forward guidance was shifted to "on hold" following three rate cuts in the 2nd half of 2019. By 3rd quarter of 2019, in emerging market economies, there was weaker than expected growth because of country-specific shocks resulting in demand slowdown. Before COVID-19, World economy was expected to grow at 3.3% in 2020 and at 3.4% in 2021.

After COVID-19, In 2020, global GDP is expected to contract to -3% from 2.9% a year before. Total loss of around 6% of global GDP. This is the immediate global economic cost of COVID-19. If we take average global GDP in 2019 as $86 trillion then economic cost of 6% translates into $5.2 trillion. It is equivalent to losing economy as large as India ($2.9 trillion), Russia ($1.6 trillion) and Saudi Arabia ($0.78 trillion) combined from the global map.

Global GDP is expected to rebound sharply to 5.8% in 2021 after COVID-19 pandemic by the help of fiscal and monetary support provided by most of the countries. This government spending is again going to happen through debt and deficit spending.

But scale of such govt spending is going to be much larger (at least 2 times) than what we had witnessed during post-GFC period. If we expect this spending to be 5% of global GDP (global response to GFC was almost 2% of global GDP as stimulus spending).

Because of such a larger scale of fiscal and monetary support, global average growth rate is going to be much lower than its pre-COVID19 level of 3.5%, once fiscal consolidation exercise is undertaken (i.e. economic stimulus is withdrawn). I expect it to be closer to 3% or below from 2022 onwards.

Total approximate economic cost of COVID-19 will be immediate global economic cost (6% of GDP) + change in stabilised growth rates from 2022 onwards vis-à-vis pre-COVID-19 stabilised growth rate (0.5% of GDP each year for at least 5 years) = 6 + 2.5 = 8.5% of GDP over a period of 5 years. It comes to around $7.5 trillion (around 2.5 times the size of Indian economy).

Impact of COVID-19 on GDP Growth – Advanced Economies (G-7)

If we go back into history (described in detail in further chapters) and analyse the impact of previous Pandemics (1918, 1957 and 1968 Pandemics) then we will find that industrialised nation (i.e. developed markets) had been the worst lot in terms of the actual damage to the economy. Given the larger size of the economy, Pandemic is expected to impact these countries very severely.

Below is the historical average annual GDP growth rate of G7 countries since 2007.

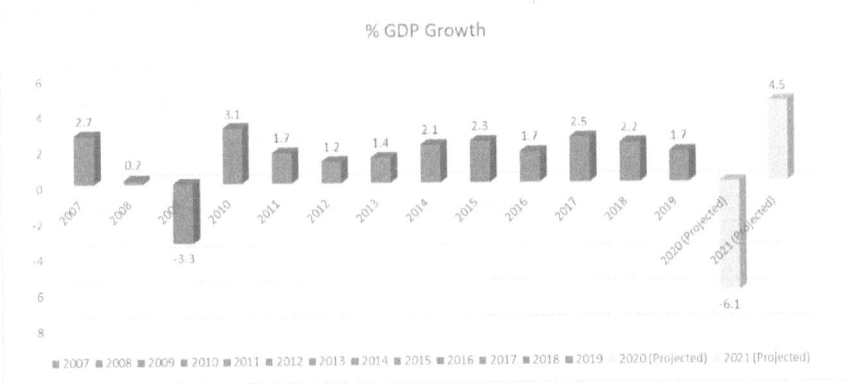

Source: IMF

Before 2008-09 global financial crisis (GFC) had hit advanced economies, the growth rate was averaging at close to 2.5-3%. GFC impact was not immediate on advanced economies. It took 2 years to see the decline in GDP Growth rate from 2.5%+ to below zero growth rate (-3.3%).

Advanced economies growth rebounded sharply in 2010(a year after GFC crisis) to pre-GFC growth rate of above 3.1%. But average growth rate couldn't reach pre-COVID19 level of 2.5%+ rate after GFC. Reason of sudden spike in GDP in 2010(to 3.1% from -3.3%) was huge economic stimulus measures undertaken globally by most of the countries.

2-3 years after 2009 crisis, advanced economies growth rate was seen to be stabilising at close to 2% rate (0.5% less than pre-GFC period rate). Reason for lower average growth rate (2%) after 2012 onwards was fiscal consolidation measures undertaken by many countries to reduce the debt and fiscal deficit in a phased manner.

When COVID-19 had hit us, the average GDP growth rate of G7 countries was stabilising at close to 2% level. But just a year before this COVID-19 pandemic (i.e. in 2019), the advanced economies growth was already in slowdown phase (a fall of 0.3% from average growth rate of 2%). In order to fight the slowdown, many countries started monetary policy easing in the 2nd half of 2019. It resulted in adding additional 0.5% growth in 2019 and expected to add additional 0.5% to 2010 growth rate (Had COVID-19 didn't happen). US Fed's forward guidance was shifted to "on hold" following three rate cuts in the 2nd half of 2019. Before COVID-19, advanced economies were expected to grow at 1.9% in 2020 and at 1.4% in 2021.

After COVID-19, In 2020, advanced economies GDP is expected to contract to -6.1% from 1.7% a year before. Total loss of around 7.8% of advanced economies GDP. This is the immediate advanced economies economic cost of COVID-19. This is the growth rate of almost 5 years for advanced economies. So, we lost those 5 years.

Advanced economies GDP is expected to rebound sharply to 4.5% in 2021 after COVID-19 pandemic by the help of fiscal and monetary support provided by most of the countries. This government spending is again going to happen through debt and deficit spending. But scale of such govt spending is going to be much larger (at least 3 times) than what we had witnessed during post-GFC period. This spending level is expected to be close to be 7.5% of advanced economies GDP (global response to GFC was almost 2% of its GDP as stimulus spending).

Because of such a larger scale of fiscal and monetary support, advanced economies stabilised global growth rate is going to be much lower than 2% once fiscal consolidation exercise is undertaken. I expect it to be closer to 1-1.5% from 2022 onwards.

Total approximate economic cost of COVID-19 will be immediate advanced economies economic cost (7.5% of GDP) + change in stabilised growth rates from 2022 onwards vis-à-vis pre-COVID-19 stabilised growth rate (0.75% of GDP each year for at least 5 years) = 7.5 + 3.75 = 11.25% of GDP over a period of 5 years.

Impact of COVID-19 on GDP Growth – Emerging Markets (EM)

If we go back into history (described in detail in further chapters) and analyse the impact of previous Pandemics (1918, 1957 and 1968 Pandemics) then we will find that Emerging Markets countries are quite vulnerable to such Pandemic. Human capital damage in such economies is expected to be overwhelming. Given the low-base effect of its economic size, economic damage in terms of reduction in GDP growth rate may not be as severe as its advanced economies counterparts.

Smart money (pension funds, hedge funds, sovereign funds and other large money managers) perceives these economies as their growth drivers of overall return on its global investment. So, if risk-adjusted return of these economies is less than the cost of the capital of the smart money then money will stop flowing into these economies. Reduction in fund-flow into these economies will have a catastrophic effect on its further growth.

That is the reason that each percentage drop of GDP growth in these economies is very crucial.

Below is the historical average annual GDP growth rate of Emerging Markets economies since 2007.

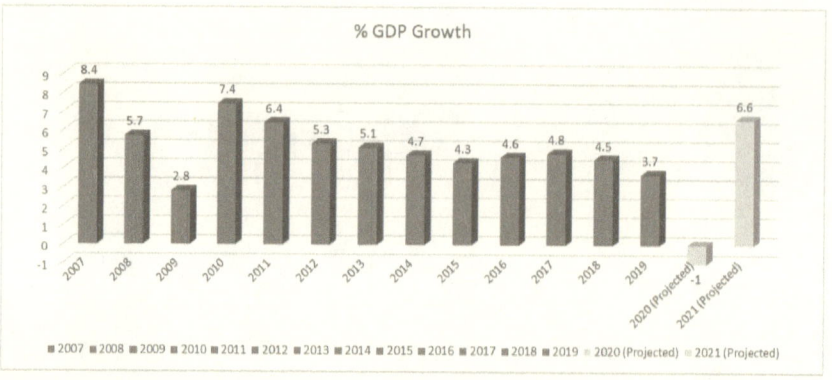

Source: IMF

Before 2008-09 global financial crisis (GFC) had hit us, the EM economies growth rate was averaging at close to 8-8.5%. GFC impact was not immediate on EM economies. It took 2 years to see the decline in GDP

Growth rate from 8%+ to 2.8%. Citing low base effect of the size the EM economy, growth rate of even 2.8% seems to be very worrying situation to be in.

It is estimated that every 1% GDP growth loss in the global GDP results in 14 million addition into poverty zone (major chunks of them in EM economies). The 1998 recession rendered 50% of Indonesia's population to poverty while urban poverty doubled in South Korea, India was equally affected. Recession also causes expansion of the informal sector in EM economies.

EM economies growth rebounded sharply in 2010(a year after GFC crisis) to pre-GFC growth rate of above 7%. But growth rate couldn't get stabilised at 8%+ rate after GFC. We never saw any year (post GFC) having growth rate above 8% rate. Reason of sudden spike in GDP (to 7.4% from 2.8%) in 2010 was huge economic stimulus measures undertaken globally by most of the countries. Most of such plans were based on Keynesian theory of deficit spending (increase the fiscal deficit for few years to support the fall in demand by Govt spending).

2-3 years after 2009 crisis, EM economies growth rate was seen to be stabilising at close to 4.5-5% rate (3% less than pre-GFC period rate). Reason for lower average growth rate (4.5-5%) after 2012 onwards was fiscal consolidation measures undertaken by many countries to reduce the debt and fiscal deficit in a phased manner.

Before COVID-19 had hit us, the GDP growth rate of EM economies was averaging at close to 4.5-5% level. But just a year before this crisis (i.e. in 2019), the EM economies growth was already in slowdown phase (a fall of 0.8% from average growth rate of 4.5-5%). In order to fight the slowdown, many countries started monetary policy easing in the 2nd half of 2019. It resulted in adding additional 0.5% growth in 2019 and expected to add additional 0.5% to 2010 growth rate (Had COVID-19 didn't happen).

Before COVID-19, EM economies were expected to grow at 4.8% in 2020 and at 4.8% in 2021. After COVID-19, In 2020, EM economies' GDP are expected to contract to -1% from 3.7% a year before. Total loss of around 4.7% of GDP of EM economies. This is the immediate economic cost of COVID-19 for EM economies. This is the growth rate of almost 1.5 years for EM economies. So, we lost those 1.5 years. Since inequality is quite high in EM economies, even 0.5% drop in GDP is going to have very severe impact on its common people.

EM economies GDP is expected to rebound sharply to 6.6% in 2021 after COVID-19 pandemic by the help of fiscal and monetary support provided by most of the countries. This government spending is again going to happen through debt and deficit spending. But scale of such govt spending is going to be much larger (at least 1.5 times) than what we had witnessed during post-GFC period. This spending level is expected to be close to be 3.5% of EM economies GDP (global response to GFC was almost 2% of its GDP as stimulus spending).

Because of such a larger scale of fiscal and monetary support, EM economies stabilised global growth rate is going to be much lower than 4.5-5% once fiscal consolidation exercise is undertaken. I expect it to be closer to 3% from 2022 onwards.

Total approximate economic cost of COVID-19 will be immediate EM economies economic cost (4.7% of GDP) + change in stabilised growth rates from 2022 onwards vis-à-vis pre-COVID-19 stabilised growth rate (1.5% of GDP each year for at least 5 years) = 4.7 + 7.5 = 12% of GDP over a period of 5 years.

Potential or Indirect Economic Costs

So far, we understood the direct economic costs, which can be measured directly through drop in annual GDP growth rate. But GDP growth rate (because of its own limitations) would not be able to capture the extent of damage that this pandemic can potentially unleash on the citizens. We will try to see those potential economic costs through country's global standings on three important parameters –

- GINI Ratio/Coefficient (GINI Index)
- Percentage of Informal employment
- HAQ Index (Healthcare Access & Quality Index)

These are fundamental parameters to assess the country's robustness and resourcefulness. The improvement in country's standings on these parameters can't happen overnight. It takes lots of time and perseverance to improve the country's standings.

An abysmal performance on these parameters reflects very poorly on the country's competence and its resolve to tackle any adverse situation such as Pandemic.

A drop in GDP growth rate captures the immediate impact on its economic activities because of adverse situation such as Pandemic but it fails to pin-point on potential and sustained damage on society because of country's structural weakness.

When economic activities get stalled because of the unprecedented level of containment measures in a country (to contain the spread of virus) during the pandemic, then a sharp fall in GDP reflects the ground reality of decrease in economic activity. But once such containment level is partially lifted in a country, then GDP growth rate may show a sharp increase in economic activity but in reality, the economic malaise remains there for a longer time in the country. Such economic malaise is more conspicuous for a country, whose standings on the above mentioned three parameters are abysmally low.

So, a sudden increase in GDP growth rate just tries to apply a mask on the face of country's economic malaise which can only be improved through a sustained and long-term effort.

GINI Ratio/Coefficient (GINI Index)

This ratio measures the dispersion of Income or Wealth distribution of a country's residents. It is the most widely used measures for representing inequality in a country. A Gini Ratio of 100 for a country expresses maximum possible inequality (i.e. one person has all the wealth while the other has none). So, the lower the value the better placed the nation is, in terms of the income inequality.

We will see next how different group of countries are placed at on inequality parameters, as measured through GINI Coefficient.

Advanced Economies (G7)

Each year's data point in the below diagram represents the average GINI Index of 7 member countries of G7 group. So, the graph shows how G-7 country group, as a whole, has fared on the inequality parameter, as measured through GINI Coefficient.

The above diagram has a declining trend of GINI Index from year 2008 to 2018. It signifies that dispersion of income or income inequality situation is getting slightly better in G7 nations over these periods.

So, in terms of impact of COVID-19, what this graph is trying to covey us –

- Lower strata of the society of G7 countries are in a slightly better condition now compared to what they were 12 years back.
- With a stay-home notice by government in many countries and a complete lockdown situation in few other countries, the lower income group in G-7 countries will have a comparatively lesser impact of COVID-19 now, compared to, if Pandemic had hit them in 2008.

Emerging Markets (India & China)

Each year's data point in the below diagram represents the average GINI Index of India and China (two leading emerging market countries) as a group. So, the graph shows how Emerging Market countries, as a whole, has fared on the inequality parameter, as measured through GINI Coefficient.

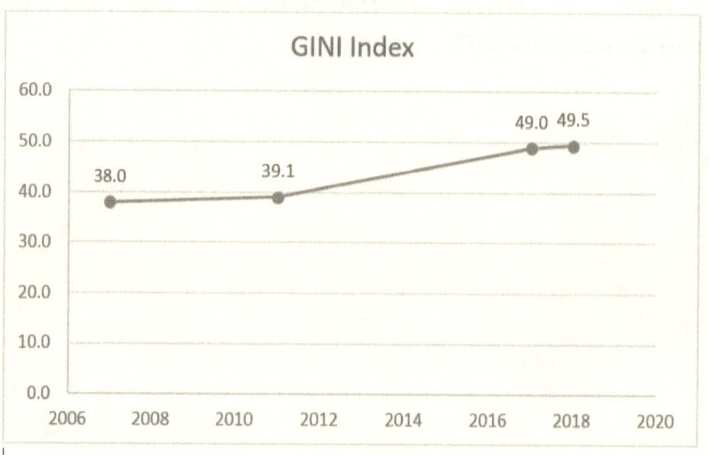

An increasing trend signifies that the income dispersion or income inequality situation has gotten worst from 2008 to 2018 for emerging markets.

So, in terms of impact of COVID-19, this graph is trying to covey us that –

- Lower strata of the society of India and China are in a slightly worse condition now compared to what they were 12 years back.

- With stay-home notice by government in some countries and a complete lockdown situation in few other countries, lower strata or lower income group will have comparatively more impact of COVID-19 now, compared to, if Pandemic had hit them in 2008.
- In absence of any regular source of income during COVID-19, the lower income group will need to depend on government's support for their survival in emerging market countries.
- A severe Pandemic such as COVID-19, stalls most of the economic activities. It results in huge impact of employment of contract and lower income groups. Such Pandemic usually lasts for more than a year (as the past pandemic did).

No income source for such a long period of time may take a toll on the lower income group, who usually don't have any savings.

Percentage of Informal Employment

All private enterprises which are not registered, and which produce at least some of their goods and services for sale are clubbed as an informal segment of the economy. People engaged in such informal segment do not have any protection such as contract of employment, wage slips, social insurance, etc. So, people working in these segments are usually quite vulnerable.

We will see next how different group of countries are placed at on informal employment parameters, as measured through % employment in informal sector.

Global Economies

On overall level about 60% of all workers are in informal sector (including agriculture) and remaining 40% in formal sector. Share of informal employment is quite diverse across developed Vs emerging markets economies within G20 member nations. This ranges from 20% of total employment to 85% in India and Indonesia.

Worldwide Informal Employment

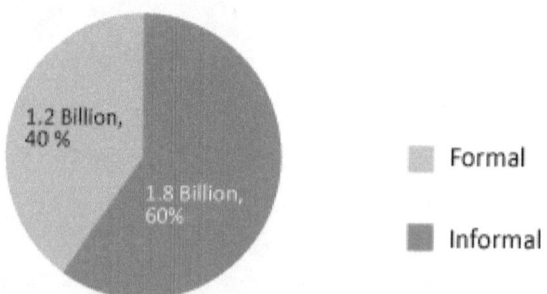

With 60% global workforce in informal sectors, impact of COVID-19 pandemic is bound to be quite severe on these segments of people. This segment would not be able to find work during the prevailing lockdown like situation. Unless they are supported by governments, they will not be able to cope up with this situation with their low or almost nil savings.

This act of welfare by government to support this segment of people, is going to increase the economic cost of Covid-19 pandemic for these countries.

G-20 Economies

For G-20 nations, informal employment is more prevalent within the Lower-middle income countries (e.g. Indonesia, India). Informal segment is at a whopping 85% level in this income group of countries.

Upper-middle income group of countries are relatively well-placed. Their informal segment average stands at 50% level.

High income group of countries are best places amongst all. Their informal segment average stands at 17% level.

This above assessment gives some perspective that how much vulnerable the lower-middle income group of countries are, in the aftermath of COVID-19 pandemic. So, impact of COVID-19 Pandemic is bound to be very catastrophic for lower income group countries.

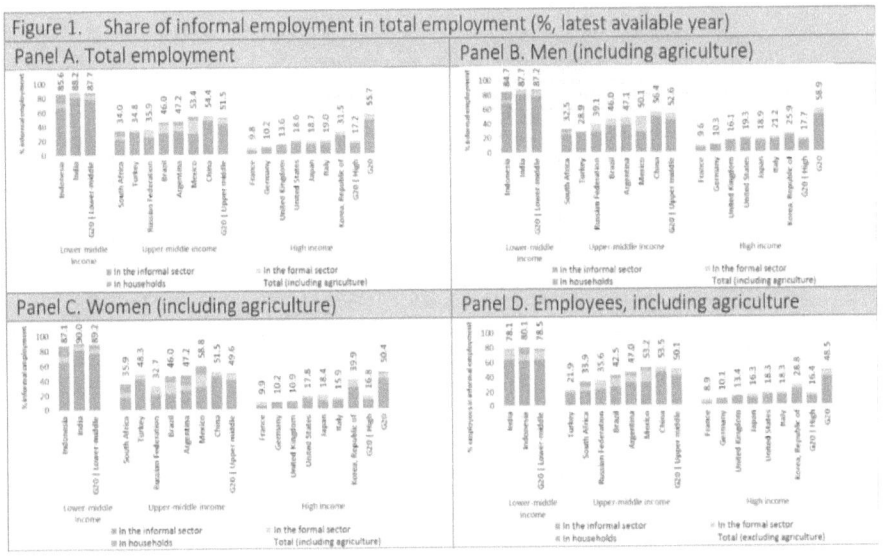

Figure 1. Share of informal employment in total employment (%, latest available year)

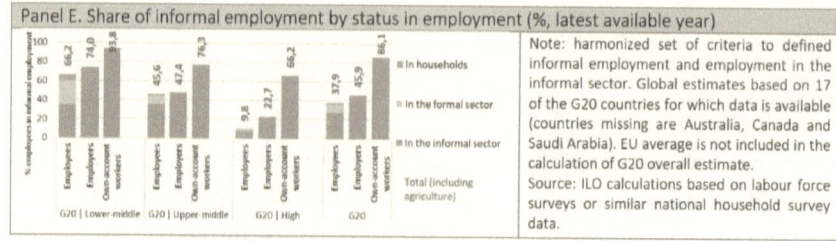
Selected Asian countries

Developed Asian countries are well placed compared to developing Asian countries. We can see Japan, South Korea and China in below bar chart that their Informal sector employment is less than 50% level.

While developing countries such as Laos, India and Pakistan are at the top of the chart. Their informal sector employment is more than 75% level.

Informal sector employment in selected Asian countries *(workforce, in percent)*

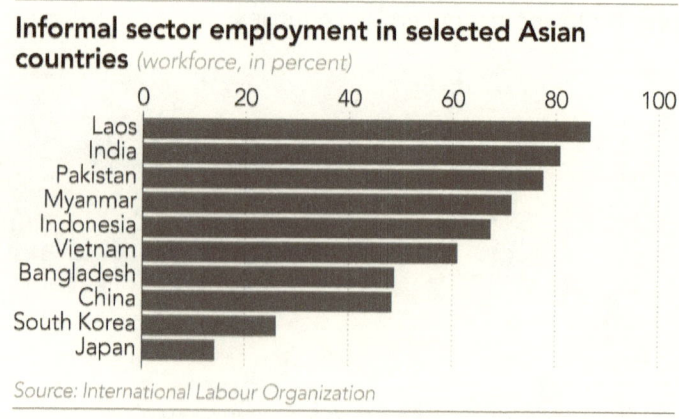

Source: International Labour Organization

HAQ Index (Healthcare Access & Quality Index)

This Index is measured on a scale from 0 (worst) to 100 (best) based on the death rates from 32 causes of death that could be avoided by timely and effective medical care.

In countries with lower HAQ Index score, we can understand how severe a Pandemic like situation (COVID-19) can become for countries. Because of inadequate and inefficient healthcare system, these countries are unable to tackle usual diseases (for which vaccine is already available), so Pandemic can wreck a havoc in these countries. Mortality rate can shoot up sharply in absence of ICU beds with oxygen or with ventilators.

Pandemic requires availability of many isolation beds (for infected people but don't require oxygen or Ventilator support) and ICU beds (equipped with Oxygen and Ventilators support). This is an additional capacity of hospital beds, besides usual beds for non-Pandemic related patients. It requires availability of additional number of willing healthcare workers and staffs.

All these additional needs during the Pandemic like situation, may turn into a mayhem. We can just visualize the problem that people living in developing and lesser developed countries can face.

We will see next how difference group of countries are placed at on healthcare capacity parameters, as measured through HAQ Index.

G7 Countries

HAQ Index for G7 countries have consistently been hovering at 80. In below diagram, we can even see an upward trend for almost all G7 countries having HAQ Index value moving from 75 to 85+ within a span of 25 years.

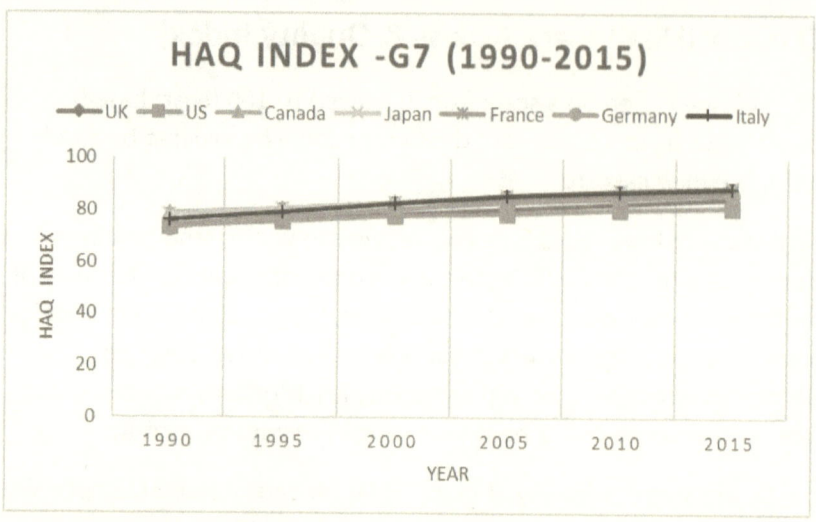

HAQ INDEX -G7 (1990-2015)

By looking at the above graph, we can say that G7 countries are well-placed to tackle the Pandemic. For G-7 countries, HAQ index has consistently increased from 65 to 85 over past 25 years period.

G-7 countries may not control the infection rate (if virus has a new strain) but they can contain the mortality rate for the mild symptomatic people by providing timely health care service. It will be feasible because of their efficient and adequate healthcare system, which they have built over a period of time.

BRIC Countries

The 3 BRIC Countries - Brazil, Russia and China have improved their HAQ index significantly over 25 years periods (1990 -2015). These 3 countries have improved its standings from an average index level of 55 in 1990 to average index level of 70 in 2015. It shows a marked improvement in the healthcare system in these 3 countries.

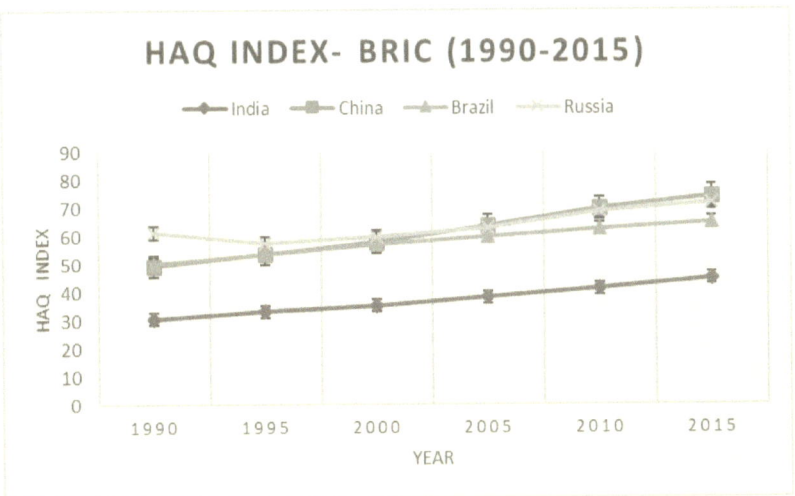

HAQ INDEX- BRIC (1990-2015)

India — China — Brazil — Russia

But India remained a laggard in the BRIC group of countries and could not improve its HAQ index much. HAQ Index level was at 30 in 1990 and it improved slightly to 40 in 2015. It shows India in a bad light when it comes to availability of adequate healthcare system for its residents.

Across the BRIC countries, there is going to be a huge strain on government during Pandemic, which calls for additional healthcare facilities to be made available in shorter span of time. The sheer neglect of healthcare system over the years, are the reason for this sorry state of affairs. But India, being a laggard on HAQ index parameter, is bound to be impacted severely by the pandemic.

Other undeveloped countries

There are a few countries, who are at placed at the bottom of HAQ Index. Majority of them are African countries. Their HAQ Index level stands between 25-40 in 2015 and there is no significant improvement in this index level since 1990. These are vulnerable group of countries.

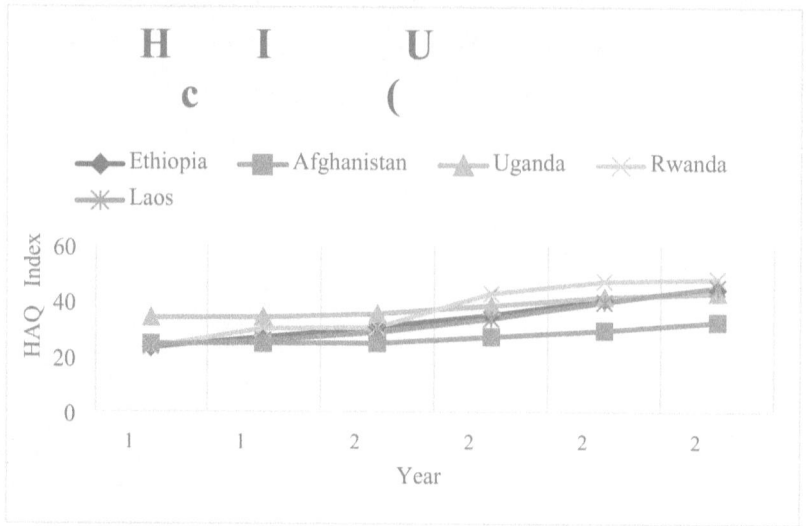

A low rank on HAQ index shows that inadequate and inefficient healthcare system in these countries. The prevailing healthcare system is in such a abysmally low situation that these countries find it difficult to tackle the usual diseases for which vaccine is already available.

So, a pandemic situation puts these countries in a very difficult setting. Pandemic asks for availability of a large number of additional healthcare facilities without impacting the existing healthcare resources being used for non-pandemic related diseases. These countries would struggle to cope up with pandemic. In absence of additional isolation and ICU beds, it may result in higher mortality rate in these countries.

Chapter-2

Policy Response to COVID-19 - US

- COVID-19 Impact on US
- Level of Containment Measures
- Fiscal Policy responses
- Monetary Policy responses
- Preparedness for Reopening of economies

COVID-19 Impact on US

(As of 1st May 2020)

First infection case was identified on 21st Jan 2020 in Washington State. By 2nd week of April 2020, US became the epicentre of COVID-19 outbreak.

1.2 million people have been found to be infected with virus. Infection rate (total sample tested Vs total positive cases) translates into 17% infection rate.

Around 66,000 people have died so far. Mortality rate (no. of death Vs total positive cases found) translates into 5.5% rate.

Average daily new cases stand at 35000+ per day currently. The worst thing is, it is at this level since last April 1st and showing no any sign of slowing down.

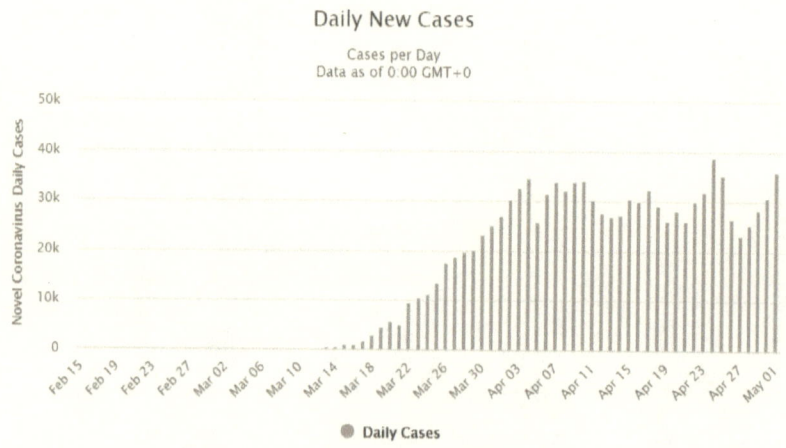

Average daily number of deaths stands at 2K per day. Average death rate is also not showing any sign of slowing down.

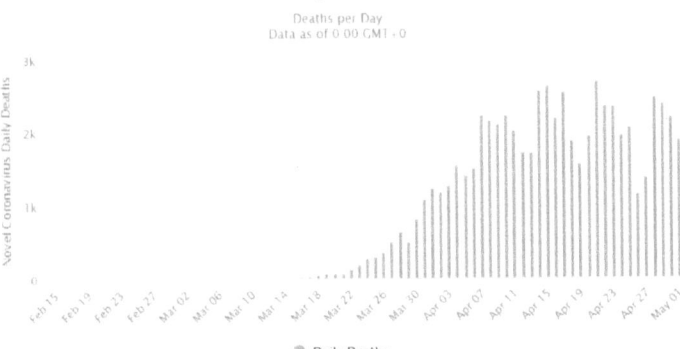

Daily Deaths

Deaths per Day
Data as of 0:00 GMT - 0

● Daily Deaths

Top 10 US states (in terms of number of infected cases) contributes to 75% of total infected cases in US. But these 10 states contribute 53% to US GDP on aggregate basis.

(as of 24th April 2020)

US States	% Contribution to nation's GDP(as of 2016)	total cases	Deaths	Tot Cases/1m POP	Deaths/1m pop	Total Tests	Tests/1M Pop
New York	8.10%	241,041	17,671	12,286	901	596,532	30,407
New Jersey	3.11%	81,420	4,070	9,167	458	164,278	18,496
Massachusetts	2.73%	36,372	1,560	5,325	228	156,806	22,958
Pennsylvania	3.89%	31,731	1,102	2,481	86	153,965	12,037
California	14.17%	30,811	1,148	787	29	246,400	6,294
Michigan	2.65%	30,791	2,308	3,092	232	102,366	10,280
Illinois	4.30%	29,160	1,259	2,274	98	137,404	10,717
Florida	5.00%	25,492	748	1,238	36	253,183	12,292
Louisiana	1.28%	23,580	1,267	5,056	272	137,999	29,591
Texas	8.64%	18,679	469	670	17	176,239	6,320
	Total GDP Contribution = 53%	% of total cases = 75%					

It implies that the remaining 25% of cases are spread across 40 other US states. Those states may be less impacted (than top 10 states) because lesser population density.

Below line diagram shows how pandemic is growing in US Vs other countries. Until the first 10,000 infection cases in US, it was behind Europe in terms total number of infections. But thereafter it witnessed a sharp growth in infection rate and become the epicentre of COVID-19 and US remained at top position of total number of infected people until May 2020.

How the US compares to other countries

Number of cases since the day of the 100th case (log scale)

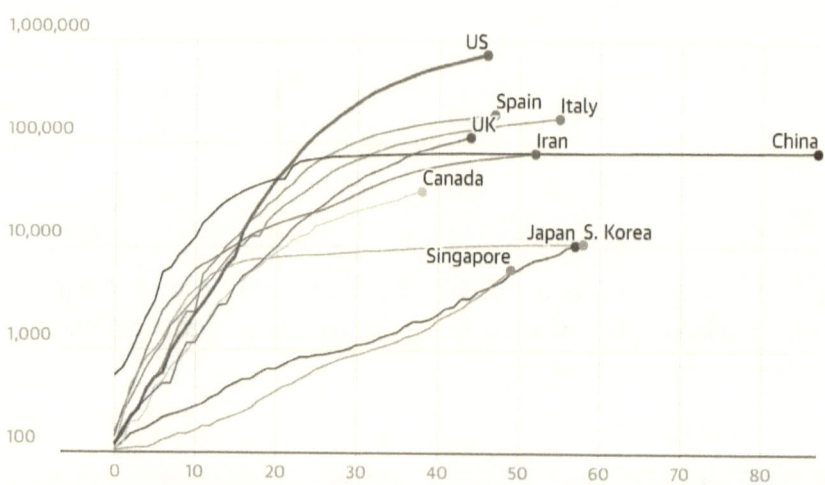

Source: Johns Hopkins CSSE Note: The CSSE states that its numbers rely upon publicly available data from multiple sources, which do not always agree

Below bar-chart shows the Mortality rate in US Vs other countries.

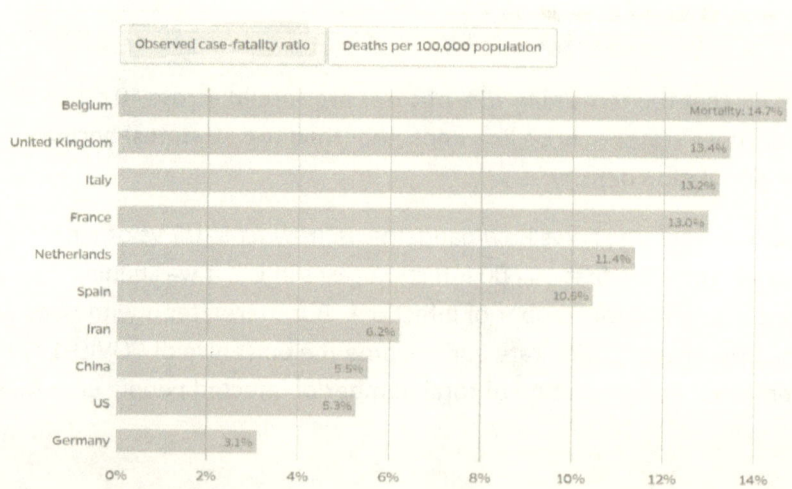

On comparative basis, US is still way well-placed in terms of mortality rate (5.3% Vs 14%+ in Europe). But on standalone level, a mortality rate of 5%

is a way too high, given its higher population compared to European countries.

Level of Containment Measures

Except for 6 US states (Arkansas, Iowa, Nebraska, North Dakota, South Dakota and Wyoming), all other US states had Shelter-in-place or stay-at-home directives for its citizen.

Residents are expected to stay at home and leave only for essential tasks, e.g. going for doctor's appointments or to grocery store. In general, walking, jogging or running is ok, but people must be practicing social distancing while performing such activities. You can walk your dog in the garden. You can also drive to and from essential services.

Stay at home notice and implementation date in all US states differs. California was the first US state to implement it (on 19th March 2020). Illinois and NJ were 2nd US states to implement the stay at home order.

State Mandated Stay-At-Home Orders by Date of Implementation

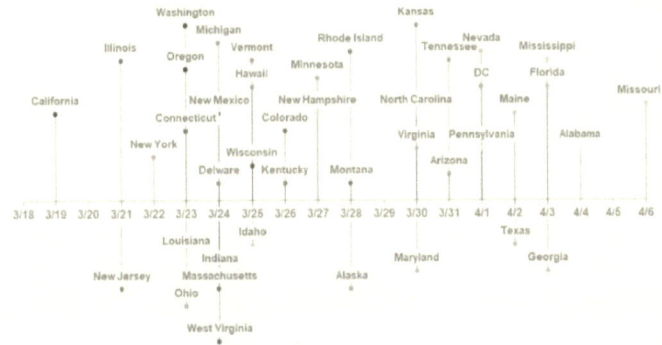

Fiscal Policy response

An estimated US$2.3 trillion (around 11% of GDP) Coronavirus Aid, Relief and Economy Security Act ("CARES Act") was passed by US Congress with overwhelming, bipartisan support and signed into law by President Trump on March 27th, 2020.

The Act includes:

a) US$250 billion to provide one-time tax rebates to individuals;
b) US$250 billion to expand unemployment benefits;
c) US$24 billion to provide a food safety net for the most vulnerable;
d) US$510 billion to prevent corporate bankruptcy by providing loans, guarantees, and backstopping Federal Reserve 13(3) program;
e) US359 billion in forgivable Small Business Administration loans and guarantees to help small businesses that retain workers;
f) US$100 billion for hospitals,
g) US$150 billion in transfers to state and local governments
h) US$49.9 billion for international assistance (including SDR 28 billion for the IMF's New Arrangement to Borrow).

US$8.3 billion Coronavirus Preparedness and Response Supplemental Appropriations Act and US$192 billion Families First Coronavirus Response Act. They together provide around 1 percent of GDP for:

a) Virus testing; transfers to states for Medicaid funding; development of vaccines, therapeutics, and diagnostics; support for the Centre for Disease Control and Prevention responses.
b) 2 weeks paid sick leave; up to 3 months emergency leave for those infected (at 2/3 pay); food assistance; transfers to states to fund expanded unemployment insurance.
c) Expansion of Small Business Administration loan subsidies.
d) US$1.25 billion in international assistance. In addition, federal student loan obligations have been suspended for 60 days.

Monetary Policy response

Federal funds rate was lowered by 150bp in March to 0-0.25bp. Purchase of Treasury and agency securities in the amount as needed. Expanded overnight and term repos. Lowered cost of discount window lending. Reduced existing cost of swap lines with major central banks and extended the maturity of FX operations; broadened U.S. dollar swap lines to more central banks; offered temporary repo facility for foreign and international monetary authorities.

Federal Reserve also introduced facilities to support the flow of credit, in some cases backed by the Treasury using funds appropriated under the CARES Act. The facilities are:

1. Commercial Paper Funding Facility to facilitate the issuance of commercial paper by companies and municipal issuers;
2. Primary Dealer Credit Facility to provide financing to the Fed's 24 primary dealers collateralized by a wide range of investment grade securities;
3. Money Market Mutual Fund Liquidity Facility (MMLF) to provide loans to depository institutions to purchase assets from prime money market funds (covering highly rated asset backed commercial paper and municipal debt);
4. Primary Market Corporate Credit Facility to purchase new bonds and loans from companies;
5. Secondary Market Corporate Credit Facility to provide liquidity for outstanding corporate bonds;
6. Term Asset-Backed Securities Loan Facility to enable the issuance of asset-backed securities backed by student loans, auto loans, credit-card loans, loans guaranteed by the Small Business Administration, and certain other assets;
7. Pay-check Protection Program Liquidity Facility (PPPLF) to provide liquidity to financial institutions that originate loans under the Small Business Administration's Paycheck Protection Program (PPP) which provides a direct incentive to small businesses to keep their workers on the payroll;
8. Main Street Lending Program to purchase new or expanded loans to small and mid-sized businesses; and

9. Municipal Liquidity Facility to purchases short term notes directly from state and eligible local governments.

Supervisory action

Federal banking supervisors encouraged depository institutions to use their capital and liquidity buffers to lend, to work constructively with borrowers affected by COVID-19, and indicated COVID-19 related loan modifications would not be classified as troubled debt restructurings.

Holdings of U.S. Treasury Securities and deposits at the Federal Reserve Banks could be temporarily excluded from the calculation of the supplementary leverage ratio for holding companies. Other actions include offering regulatory reporting relief and adjusting supervisory approach to temporarily reduce scope and frequency of examinations and give additional time to resolve non-critical, existing supervisory findings.

Regulatory action

Lower the community bank leverage ratio to 8 percent. Provide extension transition for the Current Expected Credit Loss accounting standard. PPP covered loans will receive a zero percent risk weight, and assets acquired and subsequently pledged as collateral to the MMLF and PPPLF facilities will not lead to additional regulatory capital requirements. Allow early adoption of "the standardized approach for measuring counterparty credit risk". And there will be a gradual phase-in of restrictions on distributions when a firm's capital buffer declines.

Fannie Mae and Freddie Mac have announced assistance to borrowers, including providing mortgage forbearance for 12 months and waiving related late fees, suspending reporting to credit bureaus of delinquency related to the forbearance, suspending foreclosure sales and evictions of borrowers for 60 days, and offering loan modification options.

Chapter-3

Policy Response to COVID-19 - Europe

- COVID-19 Impact on Europe
- Level of Containment measures
- Fiscal Policy responses
- Monetary Policy responses
- Preparedness for Reopening of economies

COVID-19 Impact on Europe

First case was identified in France on 17th Jan 2020. Then it spread to other regions in Europe in following order (within a matter of 15 days):

France -> Russia -> Germany -> Finland -> Italy -> Sweden -> Spain -> Belgium

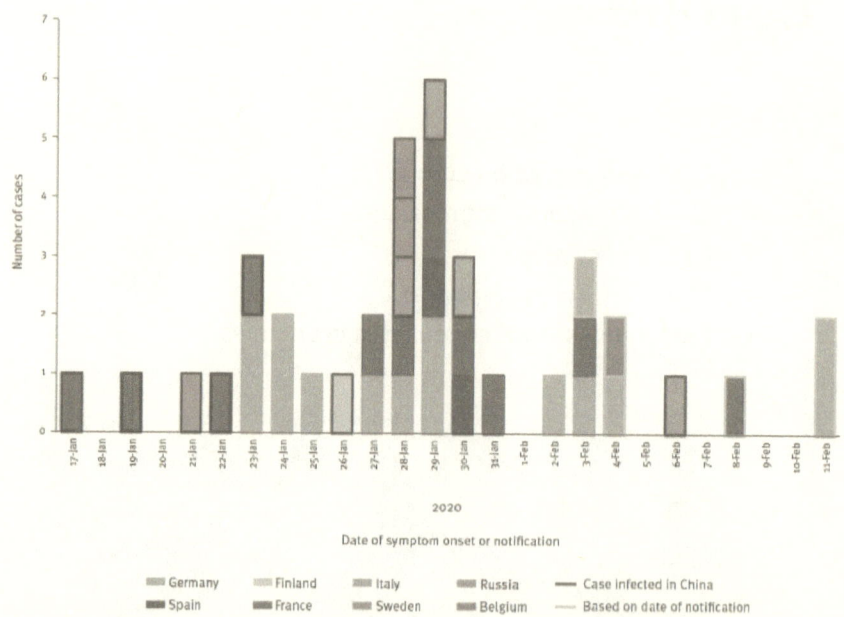

First infection case across Europe was identified in France on 17th Jan 2020. 2nd infection case was identified in France itself on 19th Jan 2020. 3rd case was identified in Russia on 21st Jan 2020. 5th case identified in Germany on 23rd Jan 2020. By mid Feb 2020, it spread to almost all European countries.

There were enough red flags for the government in each of the European countries, before the 1st infection was identified. These red flags should have alerted these government to take proactive measures beforehand.

Below is the current situation of infection across top 10 countries (based on no. of infected person) in Europe:

Country, Other	Total Cases	New Cases	Total Deaths	New Deaths	Total Recovered	Active Cases	Serious. Critical	Tot Cases/ 1M pop	Deaths/ 1M pop	Total Tests	Tests/ 1M pop
Spain	239,639		24,543		137,984	77,112	2,676	5,125	525	1,455,306	31,126
Italy	205,463		27,967		75,945	101,551	1,694	3,398	463	1,979,217	32,735
UK	171,253		26,771		N/A	144,138	1,559	2,523	394	901,905	13,286
France	167,178		24,376		49,476	93,326	4,019	2,561	373	724,574	11,101
Germany	163,009		6,623		126,900	29,486	2,415	1,946	79	2,547,052	30,400
Russia	114,431	+7,933	1,169	+96	13,220	100,042	2,300	784	8	3,700,000	25,354
Belgium	49,032	+513	7,703	+109	11,892	29,437	740	4,231	665	253,198	21,847
Netherlands	39,316		4,795		N/A	34,271	783	2,295	280	219,744	12,824
Switzerland	29,586		1,737		23,400	4,449	167	3,419	201	266,200	30,758
Portugal	25,045		989		1,519	22,537	172	2,456	97	395,771	38,814

Spain (240K), Italy (205K), UK (171K), France (167K) and Germany (163K) are top 5 in the list of total number of infected people. Mortality rate (>14%) is quite higher in Europe compared to other countries.

Below bar-chart shows - how COVID-19 evolved in Europe (across different European countries)

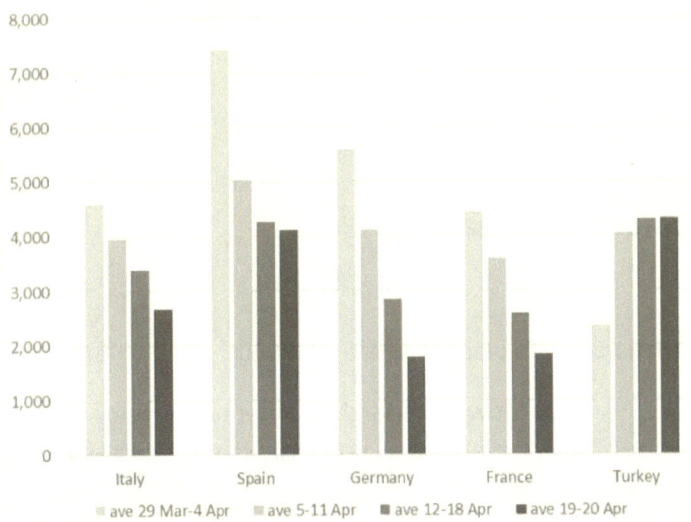

ave 29 Mar-4 Apr   ave 5-11 Apr   ave 12-18 Apr   ave 19-20 Apr

Number of new cases have declined over 1-month period (as shown in below chart) for Italy, Spain, Germany and France. But the current average infection number is still high on stand-alone basis.

Average daily new infection cases in Europe Vs US:

There is no growth in average daily rate but on stand-alone level, this current number is still quite higher.

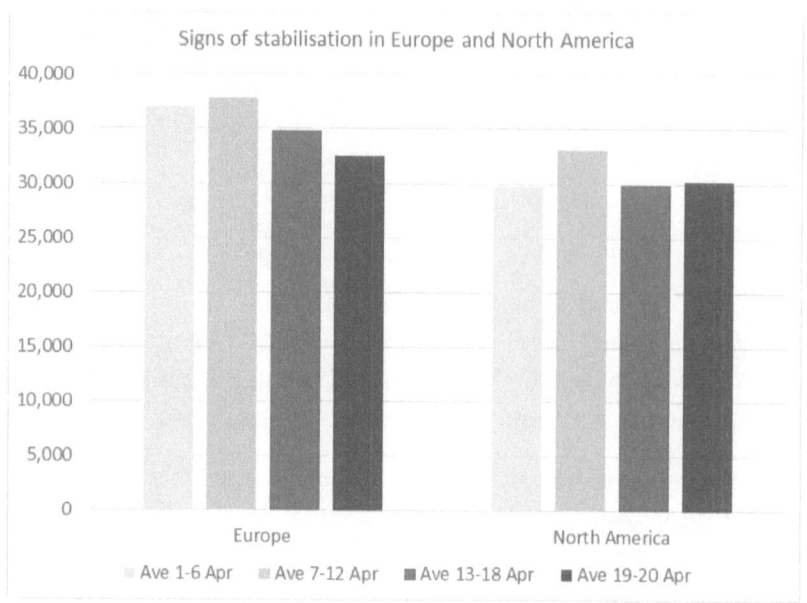

Signs of stabilisation in Europe and North America

Legend: Ave 1-6 Apr, Ave 7-12 Apr, Ave 13-18 Apr, Ave 19-20 Apr

Level of Containment measures

Italy

Movement Restrictions are in place until May 3, 2020.

Italy issued a nationwide lockdown on March 9, ordering its residents to stay at home. Schools, universities and all non-essential businesses were closed — Though, supermarkets, banks, pharmacies and post offices can remain open.

Those who violate the lockdown face fines between €400 to €3,000 ($400 - $3000) or up to 3 months in jail.

Spain

Movement Restrictions are in place until April 26, 2020.

Spain government declared a state of emergency on March 14. Schools, universities and all non-essential businesses were closed — Though, supermarkets and pharmacies can remain open.

France

Movement Restrictions are in place until May 11, 2020.

The French government announced a nationwide lockdown on March 17, banning all public gatherings and telling residents to stay at home except for grocery shopping and other essential tasks.

Penalty for lockdown rules breach are between €135 to €3,700 as well as up to six months in prison for multiple violations.

Germany

Movement Restrictions are in place until April 19, 2020.

Unlike other European countries, Germany has so far didn't have any strict lockdown — instead it opted for strict social distancing measures which were issued on March 22.

Public gatherings of more than two people are banned, except for families and those who live together.

UK

Movement Restrictions are in place until April 16, 2020 (expected to be reviewed further)

The UK government announced a nationwide lockdown on March 23, banning all public gatherings and telling residents to stay at home except for grocery shopping and other essential tasks.

Russia

Movement Restrictions are in place until April 30, 2020

The Russian government announced a nationwide lockdown on March 30, banning all public gatherings and telling residents to stay at home except for grocery shopping and other essential tasks.

Fiscal policy Response

The latest package announced by European Union of about €540 billion (4% of EU27 GDP) includes:

a. allowing the European Stability Mechanism (ESM) to provide Pandemic Crisis Support (based on existing precautionary credit lines) up to 2% of 2019 GDP for each euro area member (up to €240 billion in total) to finance health related spending;

b. providing €25 billion in government guarantees to the European Investment Bank to support up to €200 billion to finance to companies, with a focus on SMEs;

c. creating a temporary loan-based instrument (SURE) of up to €100 billion to protect workers and jobs, supported by guarantees from EU member states.

Key measures from the EU Budget (about €37 billion and 0.3% of 2019 EU27 GDP) include:

a. establishing a Corona Response Investment Initiative in the EU budget to support public investment for hospitals, SMEs, labour markets, and stressed regions;

b. extending the scope of the EU Solidarity Fund to include a public health crisis within its scope, with a view of mobilizing it if needed for the hardest-hit EU member states (up to €800 million is available in 2020);

c. redirecting €1 billion from the EU Budget as a guarantee to the European Investment Fund to incentivize banks to provide liquidity to hit SMEs and midcaps;

d. announcing that credit holidays to existing debtors that are negatively affected will be provided. The European Commission also activated the general escape clause in the EU fiscal rules, which suspends the fiscal adjustment requirements for countries not at their medium-term objective and allow countries to run deficits in excess of 3% of GDP.

Monetary Policy Response

The ECB decided to provide monetary policy support through:

a. additional asset purchases of €120 billion until end-2020 under the existing program (APP), and

b. providing temporarily additional auctions of the full-allotment, fixed rate temporary liquidity facility at the deposit facility rate and more favourable terms on existing targeted longer-term refinancing operations (TLTRO-III) between June 2020 and June 2021.

Further measures included an additional €750 billion asset purchase program of private and public sector securities (Pandemic Emergency Purchase Program, PEPP) until end-2020, an expanded range of eligible assets under the corporate sector purchase program (CSPP), and relaxation of collateral standards for Euro system refinancing operations (MROs, LTROs, TLTROs).

The collateral standards were further eased in early April. These include a permanent collateral haircut reduction of 20 percent for non-marketable assets, and temporary measures for the duration of the PEPP (with a view to re-assess their effectiveness before the end of 2020) such as a reduction of collateral haircuts by 20 percent an expansion of collateral eligibility to include Greek sovereign bonds as well as an expansion of the scope of so-called additional credit claim frameworks so that these may also include public sector guaranteed loans to SMEs, self-employed individuals, and households.

The ECB Banking Supervision allowed significant institutions to operate temporarily below the Pillar 2 Guidance, the capital conservation buffer, and the liquidity coverage ratio (LCR). In addition, new rules on the composition of capital to meet Pillar 2 Requirement (P2R) were front-loaded to release additional capital. The ECB considers that the appropriate release of the countercyclical capital buffer by the national macroprudential authorities will enhance its capital relief measures.

The ECB Banking Supervision further decided to exercise – on a temporary basis – flexibility in the classification requirements and expectations on loss provisioning for non-performing loans (NPLs) that are covered by public guarantees and COVID-19 related public moratoria; it also recommended that banks avoid pro-cyclical assumptions for the determination of loss provisions and opt for the IFRS9 transitional rules.

More recently, ECB Banking Supervision asked banks to not pay dividends for the financial years 2019 and 2020 or buy back shares during COVID-19 pandemic, from which the conserved capital should be used to support households, small businesses and corporate borrowers and/or to absorb losses on existing exposures to such borrowers. The ECB-Banking Supervision also provided some temporary capital relief for market risk by adjusting the prudential floor to banks' current minimum capital requirement.

Chapter-4

Policy Response to COVID-19 - Emerging Market Countries

- COVID-19 Impact on EM countries
- Level of Containment measures
- Financial Impact & Fiscal Policy responses
- Monetary Policy responses
- Assessment of fiscal and monetary policy response
- Preparedness for Reopening of economies

COVID-19 Impact on EM

To analyse the impact of COVID-19 impact on the emerging markets or developing markets economies, it is not a correct approach to take just a daily count. In many of these developing countries, it takes few days to collect the samples and completion of testing the samples. So, new infection cases that are released to media may fluctuate on daily basis. So, it would be better if we analyse the trends of average new infection cases in a successive block of 3-5 days.

Below bar-chart analyses the infection rate in developing markets for April 2020. Infection rate data has been plotted for Four successive blocks (each having average daily count of new inflection cases for 4-6 days) for 4 regions.

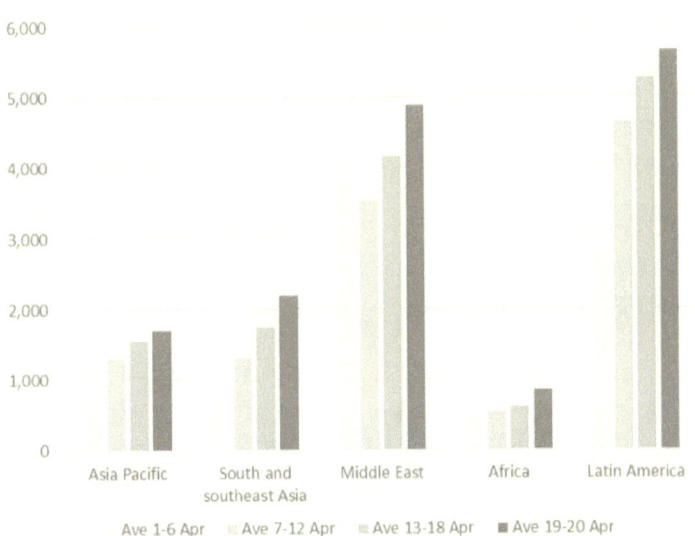

The trends of infection rate are worrying for all 5 different group of developing and emerging market economies. Middle east and Latin America are most affected regions, while Asia pacific, south east Asia and Africa are least affected regions. But this trend can change as testing rate is ramped up across the different geographies.

Below bar-chart compares the emerging and developing infection rate growth with some of the key European countries. Again, I must say that this trend is quite volatile and is bound to change as testing rate is ramped up.

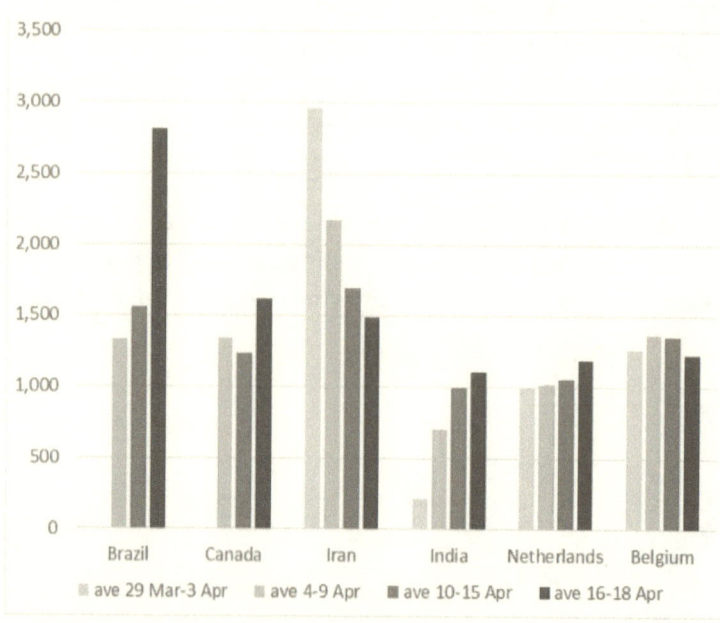

It appears that the average daily count of new infection cases is still on its upward trajectory. Though, growth of such infection cases is not exponential yet, it is still following a linear growth.

But there are various reasons for such linear growth. In many of the developing economies, the population is quite huge and dense, but test centres are not in adequate number. It results in huge amount of undetected cases.

There are other reasons as well, such as:

a. Testing criteria has a high bar. e.g. In few countries, even 1.5 months after imposing travel restriction (inbound or outbound travel), authority will allow testing of the symptomatic cases only when they have some travel history or close contacts with people with travel history.
b. Testing kit is scarce
c. Testing Kit is a bit unaffordable for few developing economies.
d. Testing kits is not adequately available across different regions within such countries.
e. Democratic countries do not want to show high number of infected cases as it will go against the government. So, there is deliberate attempts to suppress the infection figures as well.
f. In some areas, authority is not testing at faster rate (even though they have testing kits) because they don't want to strain their poorly developed public health infrastructure.

Level of Containment measures

Citing the inadequate healthcare infrastructure, many experts have advised the developing economies to have a different approach to respond to COVID-19 (vis-à-vis their developed economies counterparts). The primary focus of this approach is containment measures and aggressive preventive measures.
There are various challenges to impose the social distancing or complete lockdown measures in developing economies.

Social cohesion and social gatherings are so intertwined in people living in developing economies, primarily Africa, Indonesia, Pakistan, Brazil and Mexico. e.g. weekly attendance of a religious service is highest in Africa (80%+).

Weekly worship attendance highest in sub-Saharan Africa
% who say they attend worship services at least weekly

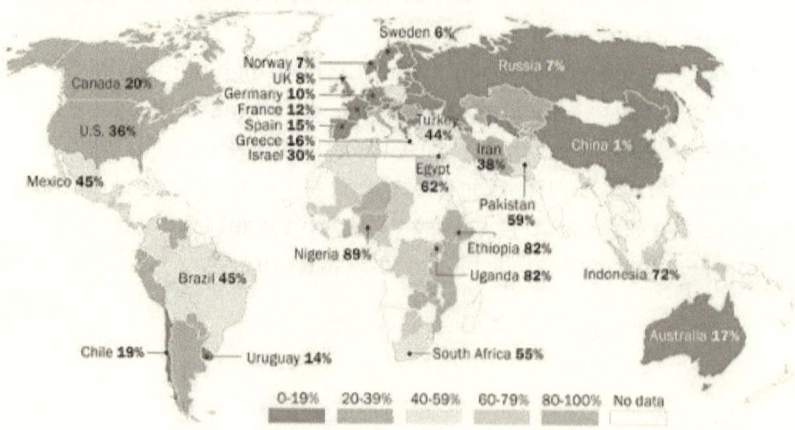

Source: Pew Research Center surveys, 2008 to 2017.
"The Age Gap in Religion Around the World"

PEW RESEARCH CENTER

India:

India has imposed complete lockdown (barring, essential services) since 24th March till 17th May.

Preparedness and response to this pandemic varied widely across Indian states. While southern state Kerala leveraged from its expertise in handling Nipah virus in 2018. Eastern state Odisha had been praised earlier for handling natural calamity. So, they also managed to act swiftly to take all necessary preventive measures. Western state Maharashtra used Drones to track the enforcement of lockdown and social distancing norms. Maharashtra used cluster containment strategy wherein if more than 3 people have been diagnosed with virus then all houses within 3km radius surveyed to identify any potential cases and to raise awareness. Though such strategy's success rate is highly debatable. Some other social challenges are:

   a. Social stigmatisation of infected people or family may force them not to report the case.
   b. non-corporation of people or society with healthcare workers (when doctors are visiting their areas for sample collection). In some cases, healthcare workers also attacked.
   c. Mass exodus of migrant workers and many who are still stuck, are starving.
   d. Non-COVID-19 healthcare system has almost collapsed.
   e. Spread misinformation related to COVID-19 is another challenge.
   f. The new cases are being twisted to fan the Anti-religious sentiments.

Africa:

Most of the African countries also imposed coronavirus curfew for different time-periods. But there were so many incidents of non-corporation, with such measures, reported. Police are using all options to enforce the containment measures such as Whacking non-compliant people with batons, firing tear gas at the crowd, using some rubber bullets in some stray cases. Many got arrested as well.

Rwanda is one of the first sub-Saharan African country to impose lockdown. Two people were shot dead by the Police, but police denied this allegation. In Zimbabwe, as well, many human rights violations were observed. In Kenya, there were outrage over Police's action. Authority have ill-planned for food delivery to people during these lockdown periods, which is forcing people to go out in search of foods or water.

Indonesia:

A large-scale social distancing measures were imposed from April 10 till May 22, 2020. It includes a ban on gatherings of 5+ people, limited public transport services and mandatory work-from-home. Authority is also planning to impose penalty on people for non-compliance with containment measures. In one of the major decisions, president has banned an annual in which people travels to their hometowns or village to celebrate the Muslim festival of Eid al-Fitr, on concern the exodus may spread the virus.

Financial Impact & Fiscal Policy responses

India:

I.   Financial Impact

India's GDP was already on a downward spiral before the COVID-19 because of its internal domestic economic woes. In 2016, it registered a GDP growth rate 8.3% then it kept falling down every year and it registered 4.2% in 2019. Now, as per IMF forecast, it may go down to 1.9% level in 2020. Moody's has projected the growth rate at 0.2% for 2020. But since this forecast was done before extension of lockdown to 3rd May 2020(currently, lockdown is in force until May 17th, 2020) and it appears quite likely that lockdown may get extended for another time by at least end of May 2020, so I believe impact on GDP growth rate will be more severe than previously thought. I expect it to close to zero in 2020.

So, there will be an impact of almost 4% of this epidemic on its GDP. Given India's GDP is close to $2.9 trillion, so impact will be close to $120 billion of lost GDP.

II.   Measures taken

Finance Ministry has rolled out INR 1.7 trillion (~1% of country's annual GDP) relief package towards food security and cash transfer, to tackle the loss of livelihood of millions of poor during lockdown.

Though, few more financial packages are on the cards but on overall basis, it appears quite lacklustre in comparison with the developed countries packages (which was on the tune of 10% of the country's GDP). But developing countries such as India has some limitation in raising funds by issuing debts in their own currency, given not-full convertibility status of their currency. On the contrary, developed countries currency enjoys full convertibility and that's the reason they can afford a huge amount of spending (10% of GDP) without any adverse impact on their currencies.

Africa:

I. **Financial Impact**

  a. Lower commodity prices (oil, natural gas, metals, and minerals) will significantly impact the fiscal position of many large African economies, especially Nigeria, South Africa, Algeria, Cameroon, Angola, the Democratic Republic of the Congo, Guinea, Chad, the Congo, and Tanzania. So, some painful macroeconomic adjustments must be made by Government at this challenging time.

  b. Africa's ability to leverage its monetary and fiscal policies for the pandemic's economic impact is limited. Whereas governments and central banks around the world have undertaken unprecedented stimulus measures, most African countries lack the policy space and capacity to do so.

  c. Net outflow in February 2020 for South Africa, amounts to 2.1% of its GDP. Its USD denominated bond's credit spread has doubled to 368 bps. Its currency Rand has depreciated by almost 25% Vs USD.

II. **Measures taken**

  a. A few countries such as Morocco, Ghana, Mauritius, and Kenya have undertaken national stimulus programs to address the short-term constraints. They have also launched the structural reforms to improve their medium-term fiscal outlook.

Monetary policy responses

India:

Indian Central Bank has announced following measures to increase the confidence in the system-

a. During the 1st half of current Fiscal year (April-September), the central government can borrow from the RBI (as short-term borrowing) as much as Rs 2 lakh crore, up from Rs 1.2 lakh crore limit fixed in March, through the Ways and Means Advances (WMA). This additional borrowing is not expected to strain the bond market.
b. 75 basis points cut in the key policy rate on March 27.
c. Raised the limits of short-term borrowings of Indian states(provinces) by 30% for the first half of the current fiscal year (it was recently by 30% by RBI, so this increment will be on top of recent 30% hike).
d. The government makes an interest payment (same as the repo rate) to the central bank when it borrows money. The tenure is three months, with a 21-day period of overdraft permitted.

Africa:

a) South Africa: The central bank (SARB) has reduced the policy rate by 100 bps to 5.25% on March 19 and then another 100 bps to 4.25% on April 14. On March 20, it announced measures to ease liquidity conditions by:
   I. increasing the number of repo auctions to two to provide intraday liquidity support to clearing banks at the policy rate;
   II. reducing the upper and lower limits of the standing facility to lend at repo-rate and borrow at repo-rate less 200 bps; and
   III. raising the size of the main weekly refinancing operations as needed.

b) Nigeria: The Central Bank of Nigeria (CBN) maintained its current monetary policy rate in March but introduced additional measures, including:

    I.   reducing interest rates on all applicable CBN interventions from 9% to 5% and introducing a one-year moratorium on CBN intervention facilities;

    II.   creating a N50 billion ($139 million) targeted credit facility; and

    III.   liquidity injection of 3.6 trillion (2.4% of GDP) into the banking system.

Chapter-5

Economic Lessons from Past Pandemics

- Spanish Influenza
- Asian Flu
- Hong Kong Influenza

There are epidemics and there are pandemics. Both are infectious but of varying degrees.

An Epidemic is a disease which affects many people within a region. Number of infected people is far more than the normal. e.g. when COVID-19 was identified in Wuhan, it spread across the specific regions of Wuhan initially. Infection was quite intense. So, it was an epidemic.

A Pandemic is an epidemic that gets spread over multiple countries or continents. So, it is the superlative degree of epidemic. e.g. Level of infection of COVID-19 that we witnessed in March-April 2020 across world, is nothing but a Pandemic.

Some Major Pandemic in past 100 years are:

- Spanish Flu (Influenza)
- Asian Flu
- Hong Kong Flu (Influenza)

There is an economic cost associated with each Pandemic. Containment measures, economic packages for different sectors, support to most vulnerable segment of the society, embracing the fall in demand and supply chain constraints.

This economic cost varies across countries and depends on the severity of infection rate of Pandemic – Mild, Moderate or Severe.

As per world bank, there are below broader impact on different regions across the world of Mild, Moderate or Severe Pandemic. This analysis is based on past 3 major pandemic (1918, 1957 and 1968).

Table 2 Possible economic impacts of flu pandemic

(% change in GDP, first-year)	Mild	Moderate	Severe
World	-0.7	-2.0	-4.8
High-income	-0.7	-2.0	-4.7
Developing	-0.6	-2.1	-5.3
East Asia	-0.8	-3.5	-8.7
Europe and Central Asia	-2.1	-4.8	-9.9
Middle-East & North Africa	-0.7	-2.8	-7.0
South Asia	-0.6	-2.1	-4.9
Deaths (millions)	1.4	14.2	71.1

Source: World Bank calculations based on McKibbin & Sidorenko (2006).

On severity level, Spanish Flu (1918) was considered as Severe. Asian Flu (1957) was considered as "Moderate". Hong Kong flu (1968) was considered as "Mild" for some and "Moderate" for few others. Number of total deaths differs in Pandemic of all these 3 different severity levels.

From the above table, it is evident that there is a varying level of impact of different Pandemics of different severity level across the world. Average economic impact (in terms of fall in GDP growth rate) of a mild severity Pandemic is around 1% across all the different geographies. Average impact of a moderate severity Pandemic is around 3% and around 7.5% for a highly severe Pandemic across all the different geographies.

The economic impact of Pandemic of each of above 3 severity level across different geographies varies. Europe and East Asia has been the most impacted group of countries vis-à-vis other regions. Developing countries have been among least impacted regions.

After observing the economic impact of pandemic of different severity level on different geographies, we will see the breakdown of economic impacts of a potential human-to-human Pandemic. The economic impact is broadly classified under 3 different categories –

- Impact due to "Mortality"
- Impact due to "Illness or Absentism"
- Impact due to "efforts to avoid infection"

As per the below estimates, most of the economic costs of Pandemic is associated with efforts to avoid infection (more than 50% of total cost). "Illness and absenteeism" make 30% of total economic costs and almost 10% cost is because mortality.

% of GDP

		Impact of:			
			Efforts to		
		Illness and	avoid		
	Mortality[a]	Absenteeism[b]	infection[c]	Total	Total[d]
		(% of GDP)			($ billion)
World total	-0.4	-0.9	-1.9	-3.1	-1,526
High income countries	-0.3	-0.9	-1.8	-3.0	-1,131
Low and middle income countries	-0.6	-0.9	-2.1	-3.6	-405
East Asia and Pacific	-0.7	-0.7	-1.2	-2.6	-99
Europe and Central Asia	-0.4	-0.7	-2.3	-3.4	-83
Latin America and the Caribbean	-0.5	-0.9	-2.9	-4.4	-118
Middle East and North Africa	-0.7	-1.2	-1.8	-3.7	-25
South Asia	-0.6	-0.8	-2.2	-3.6	-37
Sub Saharan Africa	-0.6	-0.9	-2.2	-3.7	-26

Source: World Bank.

a Assumes a human flu pandemic similar to the 1918 Spanish flu. Globally 1.08 percent of the world population dies, with mortality rates varying from 0.3 percent in the U.S. to more than 2 percent in some developing countries.

b Assumes that for every person that dies, 3 are seriously ill, requiring hospitalization for a week and absence from work for two weeks, 4 require medical treatment and are absent from work for a week, and approximately 27 percent of the population has a mild bout of flu requiring two days absence from work. It assumes that in addition for every sick day another absentee day is registered either because people stay at home to care for a sick person or to avoid illness.

c Efforts to avoid infection are modelled as a demand shock, reflecting reduced travel, restaurant dining, hotels, tourism and theater visits as individuals seek to avoid contact with others.

On a broader level, the economic impact comes from two areas:

a. On the supply side of the economy, the pandemic impacts the supply of labour, both temporarily (from those who recovers) and permanently (from those who dies). With fewer workers and hours, the economy nosedives.

b. The second area is reduced spending, that is, a drop in the demand. The prevalence of the Pandemic leads people to "self-quarantine" – they stop traveling, stop going to movies, restaurants, malls, and other hangouts places. There are severe reductions in the entertainment, tourism & travel business and smaller impacts elsewhere in the retail economy.

The global mortality rate of past 3 Pandemics is shown in below bar-chart. Mortality rate of COVID-19 pandemic is close to Spanish flu Pandemic.

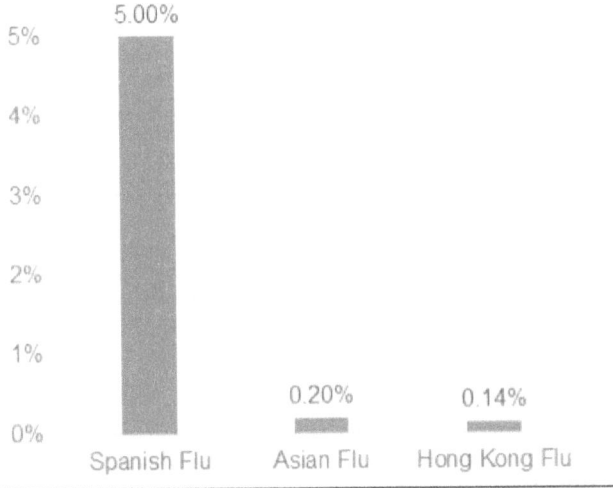

The mortality rate of COVID-19 stands at 4-5% level by Early May 2020. So, it appears that COVID-19 severity level is close to Spanish flu (higher than Hong Kong Flu and Asian Flu). Spanish Flu had mortality rate as high as 5% and close to 2.7% (50 million) of world population had died.

It is very important to understand the impact of all previous pandemics on markets. Stock Index is considered the barometer to gauge the health of economy. Stock indices changes every day to reflect the changed economic reality of the country. We will see how US markets (measured by performance of S&P 500 Index) have weathered all the past pandemics.

A severe drop was observed during Spanish flu (1918), approximately 30-40% drop. Then a moderate fall during Asian flu (1957) of 20% and mild fall during Hong Kong flu (1968) of 15-20% was observed.

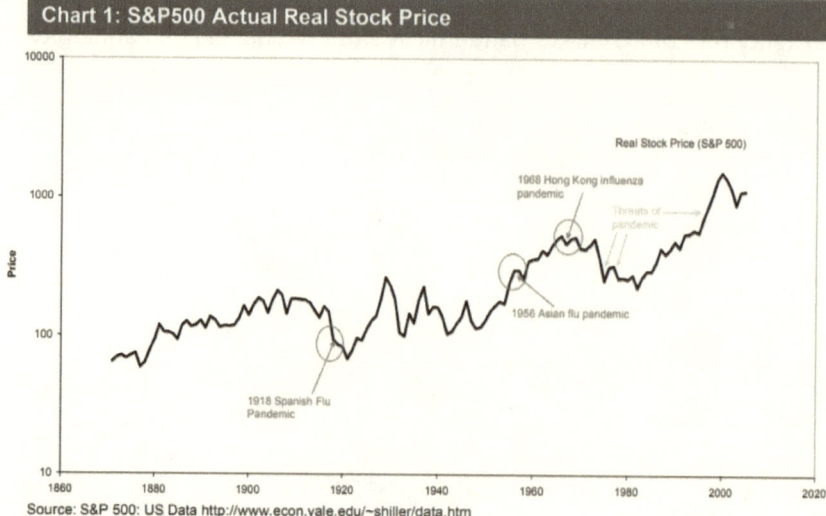

Chart 1: S&P500 Actual Real Stock Price

Source: S&P 500: US Data http://www.econ.yale.edu/~shiller/data.htm

We will delve deeper into each of the past three major Pandemics and understand its cause, origin, virus Mutation details, mortality rate, economic impact, stock market impact and many other specific details -

Spanish Influenza

When

1918-1919 (lasted for 2 years)

Originated in

Still unknown; France, China, Britain and US are potential birthplace of the virus.

Originated From

It was caused by an H1N1 virus with genes of avian origin.

First case

Military Base in Kansas, US (March 1918).

Mutation or reassortment Happened?

Yes.

During Sep-Nov 1918 (Second waves). Second wave of Pandemic was more deadly that the first wave as virus had mutated to stronger form.

There was a third wave of Pandemic too during Jan-Jun 1919. Though, it was lesser severe than the second waves but more severe than the first wave of the pandemic.

Why it was named Spanish Flu?

It was known as the Spanish flu because it was a common perception among many countries during those time that it had been originated in Spain.

Some studies say that It was named Spanish flu because Spain was neutral in World War-I (1914-1918). So, Spain could report on the severity of the pandemic, but countries fighting the world war were suppressing reports on how the disease affected their citizens.

Newspapers in Spain were therefore free to report the epidemic's actual effects, e.g. the illness of King Alfonso XIII, and these liberal reporting about the epidemic created a false impression of Spain as a hard-hit nation from the Pandemic.

How many people got affected?

At its peak, Spanish flu affected around 500 million population (about 1/3rd of world's population).

Up to 50 million people died worldwide (about 2.7% of world's population). Out of which 675000 people in US died. Fatality rate was close to 2-5% (Fatality rate of seasonal influenza is usually 0.1%).

The Spanish flu epidemic in Singapore, occurred in 2 waves, June–July, and October–November, and resulted in more than 2,870 deaths (mortality rate was close to 4-5%). The excess mortality rate was higher than that for industrialized nations in the Northern Hemisphere but lower than that for the less industrialized countries in Asia and Africa.

One of the reasons of its faster transmission was world war-I. Whole world was in the middle of the war, so it was easier for soldiers to spread the virus faster (though not deliberately). People were living in crowed and unhygienic condition too.

Higher fatality rate of this Pandemic could be due to following reasons:

i.   Hospitals were dealing with mass casualties and injuries from the world war-I, and many healthcare professionals were with the troops, leaving medical students/trainees to take care of the Pandemic patients.

ii. Medicinal Research was not that advanced what we find it today. So, quick vaccine development could not be done.

iii.   At that time, some section of medical professionals was recommending up to 30 grams of aspirin daily, which as we now know is toxic — doses above 4gms are unsafe. Many experts believe that a significant portion of the deaths from the Spanish flu were caused by aspirin poisoning.

iv.   Communication system across the world was not that advanced what we find it today. It resulted in hindrance in raising awareness among public about the Pandemic.

Mortality rate across different countries

- US (0.7 million) and Japan (0.5 million) were top two nations in terms of number of casualties.
- Australia and Latin America were least impacted territories in terms of number of casualties as well as % mortality rate.
- Africa and India were most impacted countries in terms of % mortality rate.

Estimated deaths and mortality rates due to influenza during the 19 pandemic

Country	No. deaths (in 1,000s)	Mortality rate (per 1,000), %
United States	402–675	3.9–6.5
Canada	50.0–51.0	6.1–6.3
Denmark	6.02–12.4	2.0–4.1
England	116–200	3.4–5.8
Spain	257–311	12.3–14.9
Portugal	59.0–159	9.8–26.4
India	185	6.1–43.9
Japan	368–517	6.7–9.4
Ceylon (Sri Lanka)	51.0–91.6	10.0–17.9
Taiwan	25.4–52.8	6.9–14.4
The Philippines	81.0–288	8.0–28.4
Argentina	10.2–46.0	1.2–5.4
Australia	14.5–15.4	2.7–2.9
Kenya	104–150	40–57.8
South Africa	300	44.3
British Honduras (Belize)	1.01–2.00	2.3–4.6
Trinidad and Tobago	0.30–1.00	0.1–0.2

In India, the Pandemic peaked in October 1918 and subsided by late November 1918.

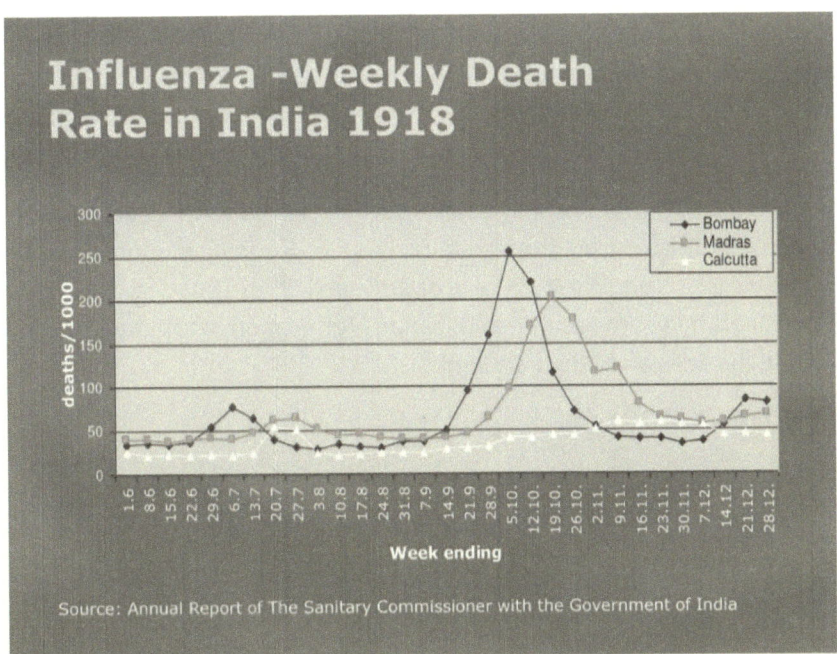

Influenza -Weekly Death Rate in India 1918

Source: Annual Report of The Sanitary Commissioner with the Government of India

<u>End of Pandemic</u>

Virus mutated extremely rapidly to a less lethal strain. This is quite common with influenza viruses: there is a tendency for pathogenic viruses to become less lethal with time, as the hosts of more dangerous strains tend to die out.

<u>Long Term Societal Impact of the Pandemic</u>

Reduced educational attainment and increased rates of physical disability

<u>Economic impact of the Pandemic</u>

Most of the analysis concluded that the economic effects of the 1918 pandemic were short-term.

Many businesses, especially those in the services industry, suffered a double-digit revenue loss. businesses related to health care products experienced an increase in revenues.

Some academic research suggests that the 1918 pandemic caused a shortage of labour that resulted in higher wages (at least temporarily) for workers, though this benefit didn't outweigh the costs from the loss of life and overall economic activity.

Research also suggests that the 1918 influenza caused adverse effect on individuals in utero during the pandemic. As we all know, an efficient labour-pool is prerequisite for the economic activities. That was the reason that it had some severe implications for economic activity occurring decades after the pandemic.

Asian Flu

<u>When</u>

1957-1958.

<u>Originated in</u>

Guizhou (China) in late 1956 or early 1957.

<u>Originated From</u>

Influenza A virus subtype H2N2 - a reassortant of avian influenza and human influenza viruses. it was a novel strain of the virus (i.e. no immunity from this virus for anyone).

Symptoms of Asian flu included a wobbly leg and a chill followed by sore throats, running nose, and coughs; together with achy limbs (adults) or head (children), and a high fever. It observed that the illness had 2-3 phases, the second being 2–14 days after the first and of a more severe nature.

<u>First case</u>

First case was reported in Guizhou (China) in February 1957. But there are no specific details on the first victim. By April 1957, Hong Kong and Singapore got affected. Taiwan got affected by mid-May. By June, India got affected. It reached UK and US in late June.

<u>Mutation or reassortment Happened?</u>

First wave peaked in October 1957. Second Wave began in Jan – Feb 1957. Secord Wave proved to be more fatal than first one.

After 10 years of evolution, the 1957 Asian flu virus disappeared. It went through a minor genetic modification, a process known as antigenic drift. It got replaced through antigenic shift by a new influenza A subtype, H3N2, which gave rise to the 1968 flu pandemic.

Why it was named Asian Flu?

Till May (initial 3 months), its reach was limited to Asian countries. Hence the name.

How many people got affected?

It is believed to have infected at least as many people as Spanish Flu. But mortality rate was lower than the Spanish Flu, thanks to, access of more advanced health care facility across the world. Overall, this pandemic caused death of around 1-4 million people worldwide. Though US Military and World Health Organisation (WHO) caught totally off-guard by this epidemic.

Mortality Rate chart – Major countries (1957-1959)

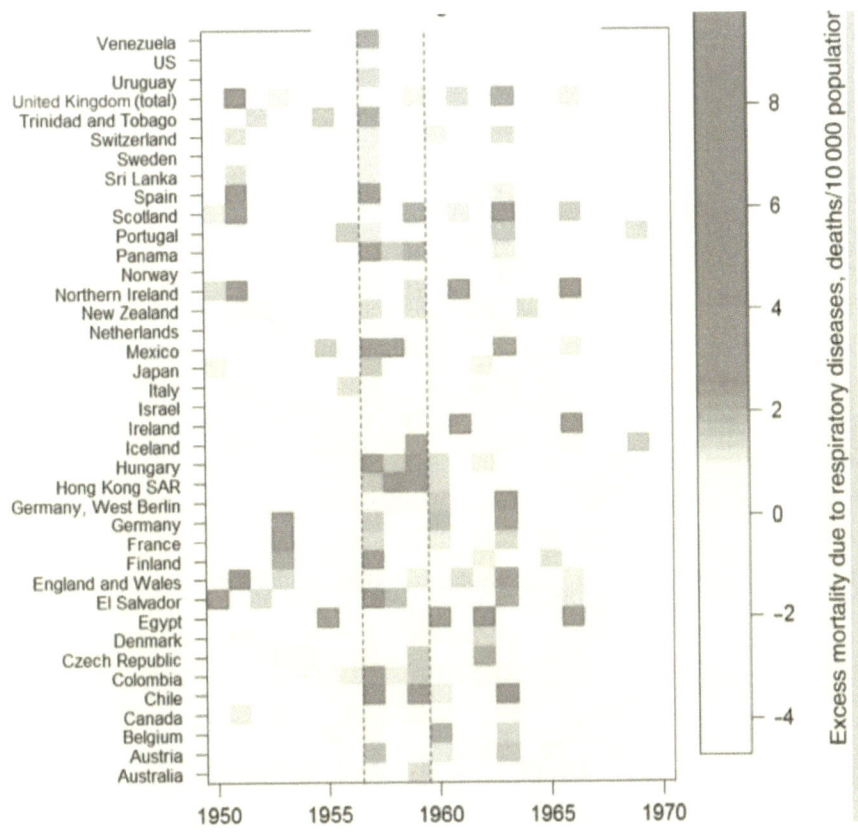

The mortality rate was quite severe in Hong Kong, Latin America and few European countries.

Those persons who were unaffected by this flu virus were believed to have possessed protective antibodies to closely related strains of influenza.

Asian influenza appears to have reached India via Madras (now known as "Chennai") in May 1957. The pandemic wave swept through the entire regions of India within the next 3 months. Between 19 May 1957 and 8 February 1958 there were 4.5 million cases reported, with 1098 deaths. With Population of India 360million (by 1951 census), the infection rate was close to 1.25% of entire population and mortality rate close to 3 per million of entire population. The disease, in India as elsewhere, seems generally to have run a mild course, although symptoms related to virus were relatively frequently seen. Infection rate varied across different states in India. It varied from 0.4% in Rajasthan, UP and Bihar to 2.8% in Bombay (now known as "Mumbai"). Mortality rate in Bengal was close to 1500 per million.

Monthly mortality rate because of Asian Flu in Singapore is plotted in the below diagram.

In Singapore, it was first recognized at the end of April and early May 1957. By May, the outbreak had become an epidemic, reaching its peak in mid-May and tapering off by the end of the month. In May 77,211 (47.6%) of 162,093 patients who came to clinics were treated for the virus; 326 of them required hospital admission, and 28 deaths from influenza were reported. Based on monthly mortality rate reports (below diagram), an excess mortality rate of 0.47/1,000 occurred in May 1957. This represented 680 deaths in a population of 1,445,900.

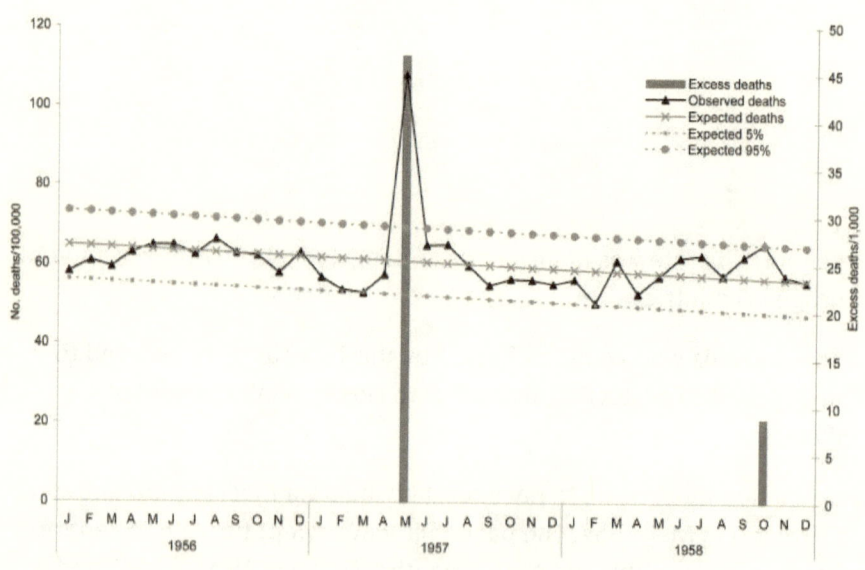

End of Pandemic

Maurice Hilleman, a US microbiologist, had made the critical observation (based on his previous works with virus) that the two key proteins in the flu virus—hemagglutinin and neuraminidase—undergo slight changes, or "drift," between seasons (this insight helped him predict the need for yearly flu vaccinations). But once he analysed the Asian flu, he found that proteins in the virus has not just drifted but it has shifted. With this knowledge, Hilleman announced that a new flu pandemic had arrived and would reach the US by September 1957. Though he met some resistance, but he managed to convince Pharma companies to begin working on flu vaccines, so that it may be ready by September.

In United States, CDC had asked six vaccine manufacturers to make a vaccine as quickly as possible. By Sept 1957, 5.4 million doses had been released: 1.8 million to the Défense Department, the rest for civilian uses.

Flu killed around 70,000 people in US, which seems to be 10% of total fatality of Spanish Flu (in which, almost 700,000 people in US died). So, early attempt to begin the research to find the vaccine did help to contain the mortality rate in US.

Economic impact of the Pandemic

Let's take a look at 1956-1959 quarterly GDP growth rates of US, expressed on year-over-year basis.

Before the Pandemic, the economy was delivering a healthy annualized GDP Growth rate of 2-3%. There was then a sudden slowdown in the second half of 1957 and into early 1958, followed by a strong recovery.

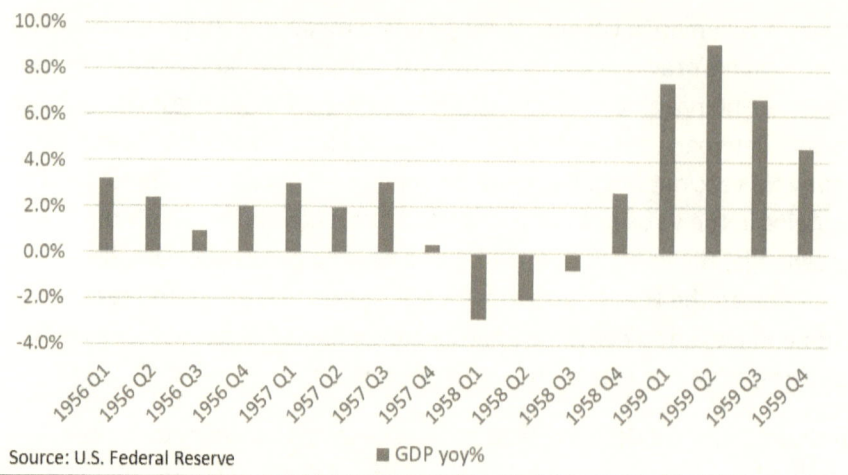

GDP Growth Around the 1958 Recession

Source: U.S. Federal Reserve   ■ GDP yoy%

There were 3 quarters of negative growth rates (Q1 1958 to Q3 1958). Though, Q4 1957 was close to zero as well. Then from Q4 1958 onwards, there was a sharp recovery trends in GDP growth rate.

Consumer spending trends (as measured by Personal Consumption Expenditures, PCE) reveals that there was just one quarter of negative consumer spending growth (in Q1 1958) during this Pandemic:

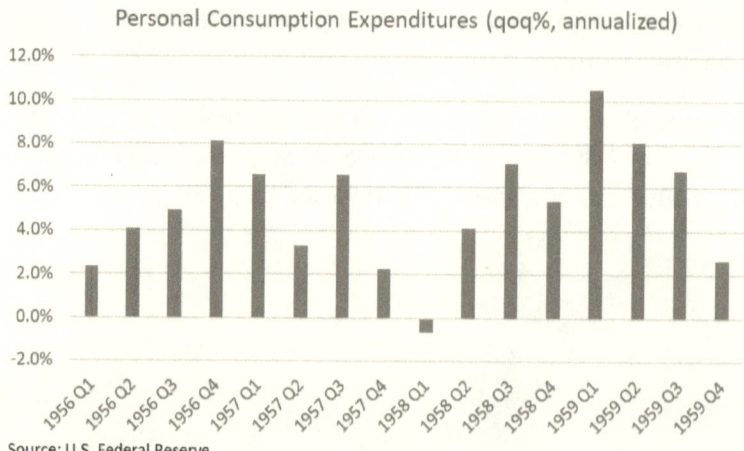

Personal Consumption Expenditures (qoq%, annualized)

Source: U.S. Federal Reserve

A Severe fall in economic activities reflect on stock markets as well. It is termed as bear market.

Stock Market (as measured through S&P 500 Index) in US peaked at 49.13 level on 15th July 1957. Then there was a sharp fall of 20% over next 3 months. It got bottomed out on 22nd October 1957. After that there was gradual recovery of market over a period of next 6-8 months by around 15%. But it took some more weeks to recover its last peak.

S&P 500 During the 1957 Asian Flu Pandemic

Source: S&P Compustat

Unemployment rate is also one of the important barometers to gauge the impact of the economic impact of the 1957 Pandemic. Unemployment in US rose from 4.1% in August 1957 to 7.4% in merely 8 months.

Hong Kong Flu

<u>When</u>

July 1968-1970. It was 3rd Pandemic to occur in 20th Century.

<u>Originated in</u>

Hong Kong in early July 1957.

<u>Originated From</u>

It was caused by an H3N2 strain of the influenza A virus, descended from H2N2 through antigenic shift, a genetic process in which genes from multiple subtypes reassorted to form a new virus.

<u>Mutation or reassortment Happened?</u>

Yes.

Hong Kong Flu pandemic struck in two waves – First wave was a bit less severe, but the second wave was deadlier than the first at most places. It returned in 1969, thereafter in late 1969 and during early 1970.

It was composed of two genes from an avian influenza A virus, including a new H3 hemagglutinin, but also contained the N2 neuraminidase from the 1957 H2N2 virus.

Symptoms lasted 4-5 days, and in some cases up to two weeks. The infection caused upper respiratory symptoms including chills, fever, muscle pain and weakness.

<u>Why it was named Hong Kong Flu?</u>

In this Pandemic, it is true that it was named after its place of origin, Hong Kong.

How many people got affected?

As per US CDC (Centre for Disease Control and Prevention), Hong Kong flu killed around 1 million people across the world. Though, it was less severe than the previous two pandemics (1918 and 1957). Almost 100,000 people in US died. Most of the deaths were confined to 65 and older age group.

The Strain of Hong Kong flu shared similar internal genes with 1957 pandemic. But still the strain was antigenic Shift from the composition of virus of earlier pandemic (1957). By 1968, there were many people who had developed the antibodies to 1957 Pandemic, this resulted in lesser mortality rate compared to Asian flu pandemic (1957).

Though mortality rate was lower, but virus was quite infectious. In a matter of 2 weeks of its identification in July in Hong Kong, some 500,000 got infected. The virus spread swiftly throughout Southeast Asia. Within few months it had reached US, where it had been carried by soldiers returning to California from Vietnam (after end of Vietnam war). By the end of December, the virus had spread throughout US and had reached the UK and western Europe countries. Australia, Japan, and multiple countries in Africa, eastern Europe, and Central and South America were also affected.

The outbreak in Singapore peaked in August 16–25, 1968. Peak daily attendance increased 65% from 6,052 to 9,966. Based on monthly mortality rates (below graph), the excess mortality rate was 0.27 per 1000 population. On overall population level, 543 people died out of total population of around 2 million during August and September 1968. Excess deaths peaked again in May and June 1970, which mirrored a possible second pandemic wave, as reported worldwide in 1969–70, although the lower second wave excess mortality rate was milder.

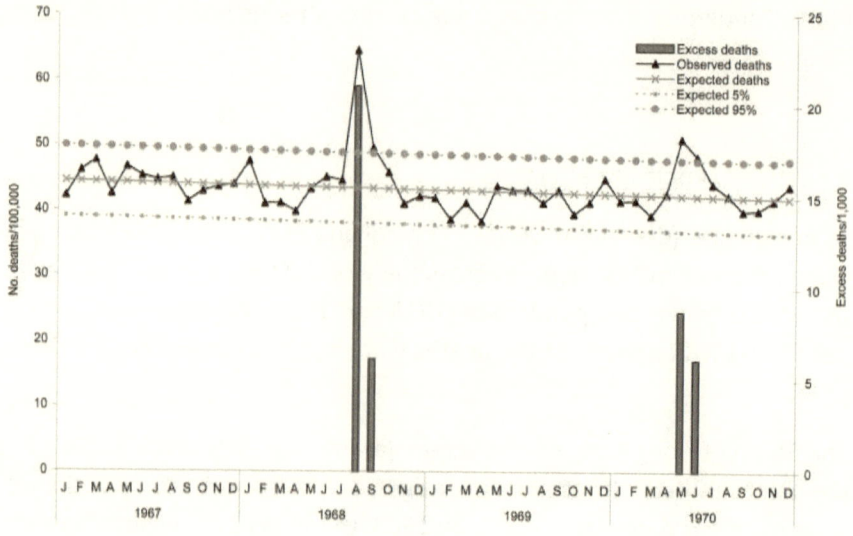

For Singapore, this Epidemic caused substantial illness and absenteeism from work. However, because of the relatively mild and short epidemic, no substantial measures were adopted by the Government. The Ministries of Education and Health considered the closure of schools but decided against it because of the waning of the epidemic.

On May 1, 1969, an article published in news agency UPI with the catchy headline "EVEN WHALES CATCH HK FLU". The report said three whales – Shamu, Kilroy and Ramu – at Sea World in the Californian city of San Diego had come down with Hong Kong flu and had to be dosed with antibiotic pills concealed in mackerel.

EVEN WHALES CATCH HK FLU

San Diego, Saturday.

Three whales at the Sea World aquarium came down with the Hongkong flu yesterday and had to be dosed with antibiotic pills concealed in mackerel.

Dr. David Kenney, veterinarian for Sea World, said the three—Shamu, Kilroy and Ramu—were sluggish and grumpy. The whales, which are mammals and subject to the same disease as humans, had blood samples taken which showed a flu virus.

Dr Kenney said Ramu had the worst case and was getting 375 pills every six hours.—UPI.

A Post clipping from May 1, 1969, tells how even whales got the flu. Photo: SCMP

In North America, most of the Hong Kong Flu-related deaths in 1968/1969 and 1969/1970 occurred during the first wave of pandemic season (US, 70%; Canada, 54%). On the other hand, in Europe and Asia, the pattern was reversed: 70% of deaths occurred during the second wave of pandemic season. The consistent pattern of mortality being delayed until the second wave of pandemic season in Europe and Asia. So, it appears that there was higher pre-existing immunity (from the A/H2N2 era, 1957 Asian flu) in Europe and Asia than in North America, It delayed the arrival of mortality peak level in Europe and Asia.

In all countries except US the disease was mild and not associated with a large increase of deaths. In US, however, the number of "excess deaths" was similar to the number in Asian Flu (1957-58).

After first case observed in HK in July 1968, a large outbreak was reported in Singapore in early August. Same month, it spread to Philippines, Taiwan and Vietnam and Malaysia. In September it reached Thailand, India (Madras and Bombay), Australia and Iran. In Japan, it failed to make any significant impact until mid-January 1969. In US, it reached in October 1968 and by Christmas, all states reported the infection. It was relatively severe in US (almost as severe as 1957 Pandemic) and it reached its peak level in US in late December 1968. In mid-January, It reached Europe.

Poland was the 1st country to get infected then it spread to other European countries. But it was reported to be of mild severity in Europe.

Some tropical countries not affected by first wave, got infected by end of 1968 or early 1969. But it was quite mild in those regions.

End of Pandemic

It lasted until 1970.

Economic impact of the Pandemic

Let's take a look at 1968-69 quarterly GDP growth rates for US, expressed on year-over-year basis.

Before the Pandemic, the economy was registering an annualized rate of 3-4%. There was then a sudden slowdown in the second half of 1968 (from 6.9% Quarterly growth in Q2 1968 to 3.1% in Q3 and 1.6% in Q4 1968), followed by a strong recovery in Q1 1969 of 6.4% quarterly growth. But it could not sustain its momentum and fell into negative growth territory (-1.9%) by Q4 1969.

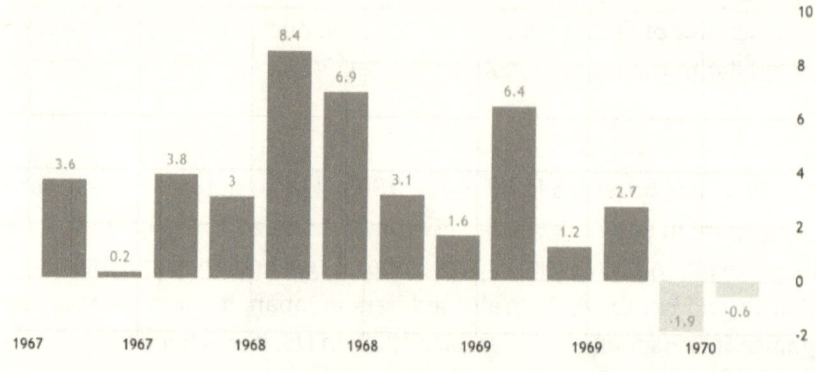

SOURCE: TRADINGECONOMICS.COM | U.S. BUREAU OF ECONOMIC ANALYSIS

Next indicator to check is US consumer confidence.

This will reveal how severely the general public were impacted because of this Pandemic (100 is the highest confidence level; which will happen in very optimistic economic environment):

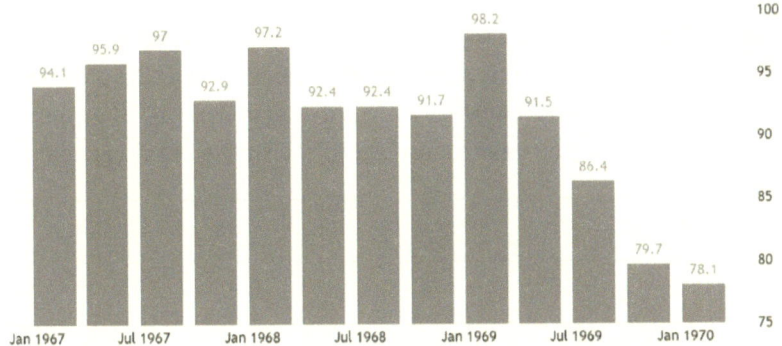

It shows a gradual drop from 98.2 in Jan 1969 to 78.1 in Jan 1970. It reflects an adverse situation on the ground during this period.

Stock Market impact

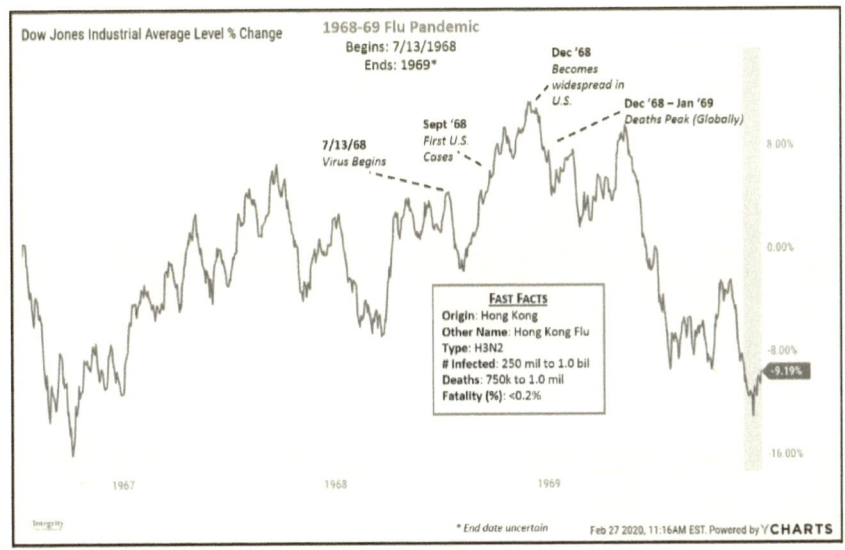

US Stock Markets (as gauged by **Dow Jones Industrial Average** Index) was at its peak in Dec 1968. During the Pandemic period - July 13, 1968 to the end of 1969, the Dow lost 13.24%. Fall from its peak to bottom level during this period close to 21.0%.

Asian markets performance as measured by NIKKEI 225 Index tells us that in Oct-Nov 1968, it dropped by around 10%. But recovered rapidly and went ahead of its last peak. It made another peak (almost 30-35% above the previous peak) on 06th April 1970. It crashed in April 1970 by almost 25%. It took another one year for NIKKEI to revisit the previous peak (Peak of 06th April 1970).

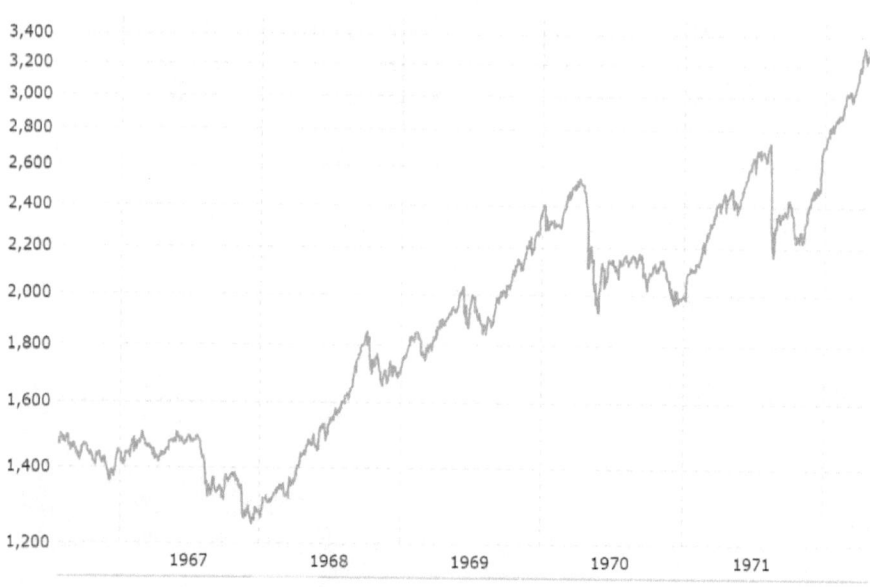

Chapter-6

Success Stories of Response to COVID-19

- Taiwan
- New Zealand
- Germany

COVID-19 Pandemic which was first identified in Wuhan, China in early January 2020, engulfed almost all the countries in the world within a span of 1-3 months. This Pandemic is being compared with Spanish Flu 1918 Pandemic in its degree of contagiousness (almost 3.5 million people got infected in first 4 months) and mortality rate (close to 4-5%). Its effect is far higher than the previous two major Pandemics (1957 Asian Flu and 1968 Hong Kong Flu).

Some countries were worst affected, and some were least affected (it could be because of different average temperature in each country during initial 4 months period). The response to this Pandemic was also varying across the different countries.

The actual objective for most of the country's leader was to reach the peak of infection as soon as possible, flatten the curve of the infection and flatten the curve of number of deaths. In order to achieve this objective, each country's leader had their own approach of handling the crisis.

Some stressed on harsh lockdown measures, aggressive testing and thorough contact tracing of the infected person. The testing criteria, as being adopted in many countries, was also one the major factors in tracing the infected person as soon as possible. Needless to say, that the faster we trace the infected person, the greater would be the odd of the saving the lives of those infected person. Below are testing criteria majority of the countries were adopting for testing:

a. Only those symptomatic people having travel history.

b. Some were testing people with travel history or close contacts with such people with travel history.

c. Some were testing symptomatic people with or without travel history.

d. After having tested enough symptomatic cases, some had started testing asymptomatic people as well without any travel history or close contacts with any such people, just to ensure testing rate per million population is adequate to arrive at some conclusion about flattening curve.

e. Some were at advanced stage after testing enough symptomatic and asymptomatic cases, planning to test human sewage to track the spread of the virus. Also, some wanted to do this testing before relaxing the lockdown restrictions.

There have been numerous success stories related to response to COVID-19. But the response of the nations that stand out from crowd of other nations are:

1. Taiwan
2. New Zealand
3. Germany

It is a quite a coincident that all these nations are being led by a woman. So, it is worthwhile to know how their approach are different from other nations.

Taiwan

China, being in a neighbourhood, was a great risk from the COVID-19 pandemic. Also, because of close ties with Chinese territory, it is quite common for people from both countries (China and Taiwan) to travel other countries quite frequently.

President Tsai Ing-wen (previously a law professor), who recently got re-elected as President of Taiwan in January 2020, took a tough decision to contain the virus transmission very early (in Jan 2020). As per those measures, the visitors were restricted from either side and new mandatory health checks was enforced.

But Instead of banning travel from China outrightly, All the arrivals were advised to undergo with a 14-days self-quarantine.

After the first imported case was identified on Jan. 21, 2020, four major airlines suspended flights between Taiwan and Wuhan. A ban on all flights except those which are from Beijing, Shanghai, Xiamen and Chengdu was implemented three weeks later.

Strict home quarantine

Taking cues from previous Pandemic, Taiwanese government foresaw that After Chinese New Year (an annual celebration among Chinese community, which fell in Mid-January in 2020), infection rate may shoot up sharply if no proactive measures are taken.

Taiwanese government did some homework and prepared themselves to tackle the COVID-19 Pandemic during Chinese New Year this year. They built a technology-based infrastructure to track the people in quarantine - A location-tracking apparatus, which monitors some 86,000+ people under mandatory home quarantine to control the spread of COVID-19.

The monitoring system in Taiwan is also known as a "digital fence," using which location of quarantined person is monitored via cellular signals from their phones. Stepping too far from homes triggers the alert system. Thereafter, calls and messages are sent to people to ascertain their whereabouts. Anyone, caught breaching their quarantine, can be fined up to $33,000 (a mammoth monetary fine).

For foreign arrivals, some state-run facilities had been used for quarantines, but home quarantine had been the predominant method of isolation (if they reside in Taiwan) even when state facilities were available. This is because of their efficient surveillance system in place for tracking offenders in the home quarantine.

If a person acts smart and venture out without his/her cell-phone, then Taiwanese police has a solution to find such offenders as well. There is a M-Police system, which was first established in 2007 and gives officers a cloud-based access to numerous databases—including, now, a database of individuals under quarantine orders. The police then fan out to popular hangout places like bars and restaurants, checking the identities of customers to see if anyone's identity in those hangout places matches up with the list of quarantined individuals. More than a dozen offenders have been caught this way and fined heftily.

If person in quarantine switches off the phone or gets switched off because of low battery, the police will come knocking at his/her door to understand the matter.

Some liberal nations may find it quite intriguing and very few nations can implement such a surveillance system. Such a large scale of surveillance can be materialised only when people have trust in their governments.

There are three types of epidemic response measures that restrict physical movements as introduced by the Central Epidemic Command Centre (CECC) based on the Communicable Disease Control Act:

- Home quarantine
- home isolation
- self-health management

The first two (Home quarantine & home isolation) have more stringent requirements and are legally binding on the individual who have been asked to do so. As a part of these measures, leaving the house is totally prohibited. It also involves a regular check-up from health care authorities. People who have been issued a self-health management notice are not banned from leaving the house but recommended to wear a mask when doing so.

Less emphasis on large scale testing

Taiwan is not adopting widespread testing strategy, as South Korea and some other countries have done. As per their health ministry, widespread testing is a waste of resources, where workers have been able to trace almost all cases and their contacts.

Such a strategy is relatively easier implement in a country of 24 million population but challenging for other populous countries such as India, US, Germany, etc.

Robust healthcare system

During any health crisis, a robust health system is very crucial to support the surge of medical care and testing needed. Taiwan has a solid public health, medical, and insurance infrastructure distributed across the country.

This infrastructure consists of local health departments and centres staffed by healthcare professionals trusted by local residents, particularly in the rural areas where private practices are inadequate; hospitals, medical centres, and clinics that strongly support a well-coordinated infectious disease network for preparedness and response; and a comprehensive National health Insurance (NHI) that covers close to 99% of the population with high-quality providers and low out-of-pocket cost.

The interconnected health system reduces barriers to doctor appointments and follow-up visits, which helped capture suspected cases with minor symptoms. Furthermore, the single-payer NHI model has a centralized health records of population-level data and the capability of merging information from other government databases. This connectivity proved a valuable tool for analysis and case investigation during disease outbreaks, including dengue, influenza, SARS, and the current COVID-19 pandemic.

Effectiveness of the measures taken

As of 26th April 2020, there are only 429 cases reported for 24 million country's population. Out of which, only 6 death were reported. They have tested 60,000 samples (almost 2500 per million population).

Total Coronavirus Cases in Taiwan

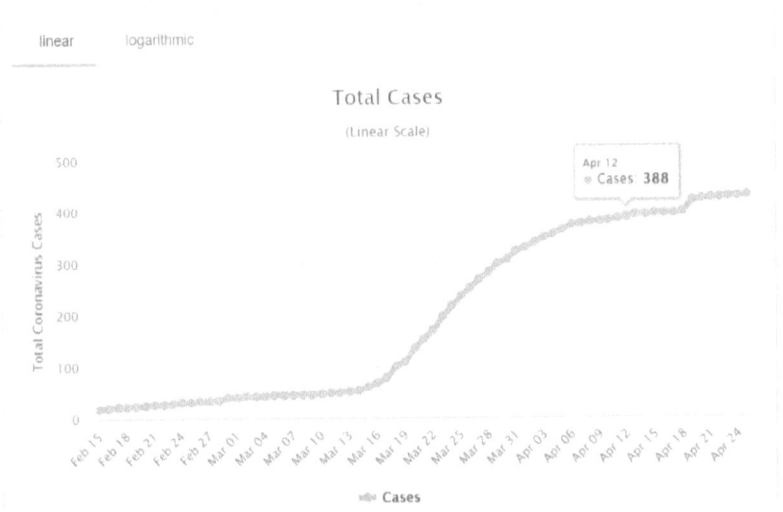

Until Mid-March 2020 the new infection cases were contained (close to 50) but thereafter it shot up to 400 by early April. After that it got bottomed out. We can say that the Taiwanese Government have managed to flatten the curve of new infection and new death by 1st week of April 2020.

New Zealand

Since PM Jacinda Ardern took office in October 2017, she has taken several bold steps to tackle the unusual situations.

In 2019, when New Zealand (NZ) was rocked by attacks on two mosques in Christchurch that claimed 51 lives, PM Ardern pledged to cover funeral costs for victims, reached out to Muslim community and pushed through swift changes to the country's gun laws.

Now, just a year afterwards, NZ is facing the heat of COVID-19. PM Ardern closed country's border swiftly. NZ has close to 5 million population, much lesser than NY. Also, geographically it is an island nation. It shares no land borders with any country, it is surrounded by South Pacific Ocean and the Tasman Sea. So, it was comparatively easier for NZ to implement the sealing off its borders.

Brilliant communicator

PM Ardern has repeatedly called the country "our team of 5 million". Since the COVID-19 Pandemic ill-effect was known to all countries, government have taken initiative to communicate many complex health issues around COVID-19 to its citizen in a plain language.

It was clearly communicated where is the trajectory pointing to in terms of number of new cases. So, when the government announced a complete lockdown to contain the virus, people understood it quite well why it was necessary to do so.

While explaining, the public in detail the rules of the lockdown and the trajectory of the new cases, PM Ardern has also emphasized on a distinguishing trait - "kindness". She has ended almost all her public appearances with the same message: "Be Strong. Be Kind". After announcement of lockdown, PM Ardern interacted public by going to Facebook Live, saying she wanted to "check in with everyone", if everyone is well-prepared to comply with the lockdown.

The general perception, about the current government, in the public is - "Every decision is made with the disclaimer that she knows how difficult it's going to be for people". She had clearly told the public that the goal is the total elimination of the disease from its shores not just the containment of the virus from spreading.

Natural advantage

Unlike many other countries, NZ has an advantage of being a remote island nation with no land borders. It also has a very low population density. Most residents live in houses on individual lots spread across larger spaces. Most prefers private vehicles to public transport. Its underground train does not get crowded like New York. "We benefit from a very large moat," Ardern recently acknowledged.

Effectiveness of the measures taken

As of 26th April 2020, there are only 1470 cases reported for 5 million country's population. Out of which, only 18 death were reported. They have tested 121,000 samples (almost 25000 per million population).

Total Coronavirus Cases in New Zealand

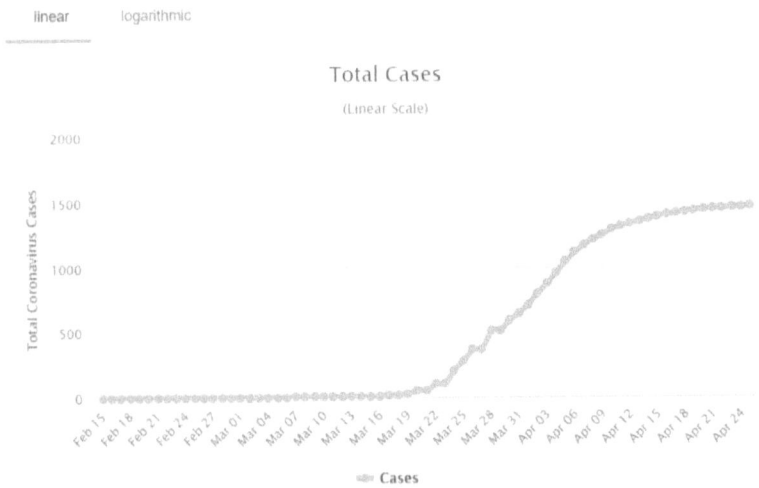

Until Mid-March 2020 the new infection cases were contained but thereafter it shot up to 1500 by mid-April. After that growth of new cases got bottomed out. We can say that the New Zealand Government have managed to flatten the curve of new infection and new death by mid-April 2020. Though, Government is not sitting on laurels rather they prefer to aim higher now. They want to achieve a total elimination of virus from its shores.

Daily New Cases in New Zealand

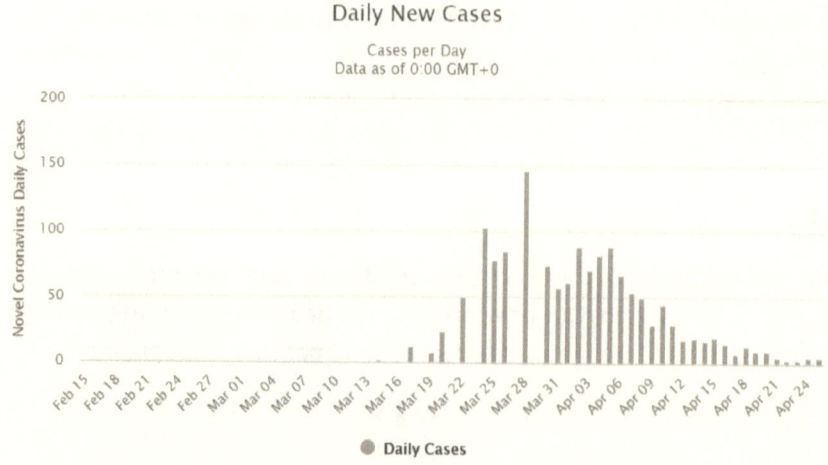

Daily New Cases

Cases per Day
Data as of 0:00 GMT+0

● Daily Cases

Germany

In 2015, when Angela Merkel completed 10th year as chancellor of Germany, she was conferred the Time's person of the year title. The leadership that she has provided to European Union during tough times, is simply commendable. She has recently announced that she won't seek re-election for fifth term as German chancellor (election is due in mid-2021). So, COVID-19 seems to be her last major challenge before she leaves the office next year.

On 18th March 2020, German Chancellor Angela Merkel made a rare televised speech in which she warned the public that the outbreak poses "the largest challenge since the World War II". It was quite a strong statement but still a well-thought one. She definitely knew what its implications are.

Transparent and empathetic attitude

"I'm absolutely sure we will overcome this crisis," she said. "But how many casualties will there be? How many loved ones will we lose?". Every death, Merkel said, is "a father or grandfather, a mother or grandmother, a partner".

"It's people," she said. "And we are a community in which every life and every person counts."

Rapid and high Testing rate

In many countries, only high-risk patients, the most critically ill and symptomatic people are being tested. This dramatically underestimates case numbers, as most cases cause mild illness and would not be tested. Germany's robust and rapid testing programme was helped by the usage of a distributed network of testing through individual hospitals, clinics and laboratories, instead of relying on tests from a single government resource, as was the case in countries such as the US and the UK.

The federated German system allows for more regional autonomy, making it easier for local healthcare systems to coordinate the work of different laboratories. As the virus spreads from people at early stages of the disease with no or mild symptoms, early identification and isolation would have a very large impact on the spread of the virus.

Robust and adequate critical care facility

Slowing the spread in Germany has also enabled the increased hospital readiness. This in turn helped in reducing the fatalities. e.g. the number of acute-care beds in Germany is 621 per 100,000 people, compared with Italy's 275 beds per 100,000 and the UK's 228 beds per 100,000 people.

Germany had its first case of COVID-19 infection on Jan 27, before Italy on Jan 31, but the first fatality was records only on March 9, significantly later than in Italy on Feb 21.

Effectiveness of the measures taken

The COVID-19 infection rate was alarmingly higher in European countries (possibly weather effect) compared to Asian and African countries. Most of the leading countries in Europe which has a lesser population than Germany (83 million) has higher infection rate and higher mortality rate.

- Spain – Population 47 million. Total infection 240,000 and death 25,000 (~11% mortality rate) as of 30th April 2020.

- Italy – Population 60 million. Total infection 206,000 and death 28,000 (~14% mortality rate) as of 30th April 2020.

- UK – Population 67 million. Total infection 171,000 and death 27,000 (~16% mortality rate) as of 30th April 2020.

- France – Population 67 million. Total infection 167,000 and death 24,000 (~15% mortality rate) as of 30th April 2020.

As of 30th April 2020, there are around 163,000 cases reported for 83 million country's population. Out of which, only 6623 death were reported (~4% mortality rate). Since Average mortality rate in other countries is 14%, So it implies that Germany managed to save lives of almost 10% of the infected person because of efficient health care facilities.

Germany have tested 2.6 million samples (almost 30000 per million population).

Total Coronavirus Cases in Germany

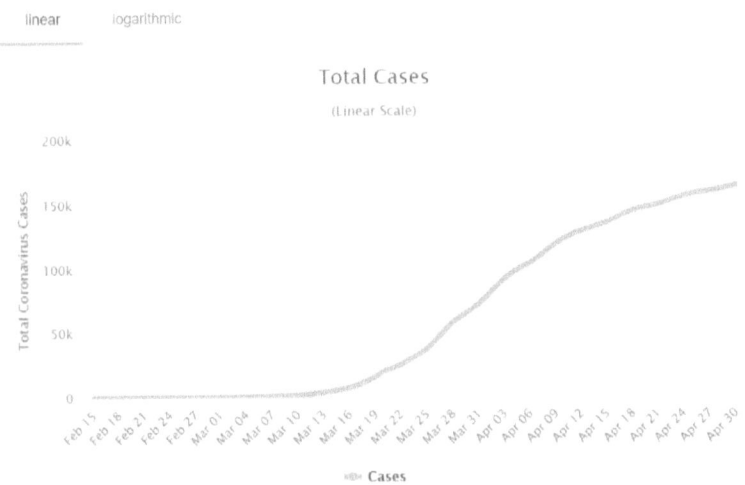

New cases started going up from mid-March 2020. Growth of new cases has slowed down. But it may take a while to contain the new infection cases in single digits.

Daily New Cases in Germany

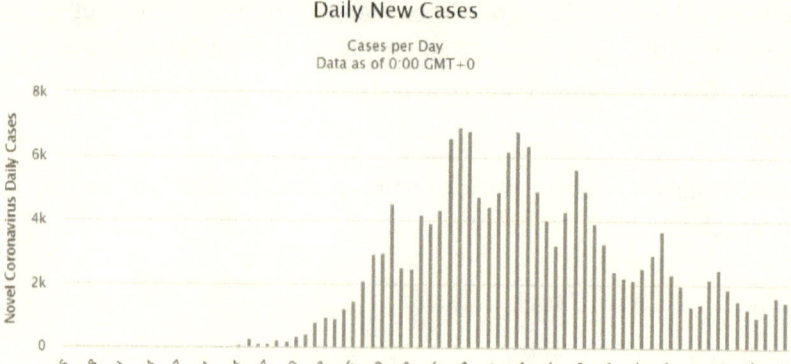

A General Commentary on COVID-19 mitigation strategy

There are many other countries whose response to COVID-19 was noteworthy as well. Few countries made mistakes in their approach initially and corrected later.

For many countries, it was a trade-off between the lessening the economic impact and saving the human lives. Few countries chose the former (lessening the economic impact), few opted the latter and few went for a balanced calibrated approach between the two objectives.

Some countries were lucky enough to have the infection rate of COVID-19 too slow without taking any adequate measures.

Some countries did well initially but turned complacent later, it resulted in spike of infection rate at the later stage.

As of now, at overall level the severity of the infection has indeed been slowed down across the world. But there is still a risk of spike in infection rate when containment measures are lifted by all the countries.

Safest way to eliminate COVID-19 virus is to find an effective vaccine. At least 102 vaccine candidates are under development across the world. Eight of them have entered the early clinical trial stage. As per prevailing process, vaccines must go through 3 progressively more stringent human trial phases before they are considered safe and effective. These phases assess the candidates' safety profile, the strength of the immune responses they trigger, and how good they are at protecting people from infection and disease. Most candidates don't make it. Success rate is as low as less than 10% of all participating candidates. If successful, then it takes at least 18 months to 10 years to complete the entire trial phases.

Also, there is high likelihood of arrival of second wave of this Pandemic as happened during all previous Pandemic (Spanish flu, Asian Flu and Hong Kong Flu). Second wave in all previous Pandemic was more severe than the first wave.

Hope this time round we get lucky.

References:

https://www.imf.org/

https://www.indexmundi.com/facts/indicators/SI.POV.GINI/rankings

https://knoema.com/atlas/ranks/GINI-index

https://www.cia.gov/library/publications/the-world-factbook/rankorder/2172rank.html

https://www.newindianexpress.com/magazine/voices/2020/apr/19/economic-shocks-to-hit-children-2131071.html

http://www.g20.utoronto.ca/2018/g20_paper_on_nse_and_formalization_ilo.pdf

https://www.imf.org/en/Topics/imf-and-covid19/Policy-Responses-to-COVID-19

https://www.worldometers.info/coronavirus/

https://simple.wikipedia.org/wiki/List_of_U.S._states_by_GDP

https://ourworldindata.org/grapher/healthcare-access-and-quality-index

https://www.eurosurveillance.org/content/10.2807/1560-7917.ES.2020.25.9.2000178

https://www.globalcapital.com/article/b1kqc2ql83dz82/the-coronavirus-graphic-to-watch-disease-moves-steadily-south

https://www.ncbi.nlm.nih.gov/

www.ingramcontent.com/pod-product-compliance
Lightning Source LLC
Chambersburg PA
CBHW020551220526
45463CB00006B/2257